TOP SECRET

DISCARD

THE
DOOMSDAY
SCENARIO

L. DOUGLAS KEENEY
FOREWORD BY STEPHEN I. SCHWARTZ

MBI Publishing Company

First published in 2002 by MBI Publishing Company, Galtier Plaza, Suite 200, 380 Jackson Street, St. Paul, MN 55101-3885 USA

MBI Publishing Company books are also available at discounts in bulk quantity for industrial or sales-promotional use. For details write to Special Sales Manager at Motorbooks International Wholesalers & Distributors, Galtier Plaza, Suite 200, 380 Jackson Street, St. Paul, MN 55101-3885 USA.

Library of Congress Cataloging-in-Publication Data Available
ISBN 0-7603-1313-X

On the front cover: The PRISCILLA test (XX-10) was a 37 kiloton shot fired June 24, 1957 at the Nevada Test Site.

Edited by Michael Haenggi
Designed by Stephanie Michaud
Printed in China

6/02

The Emergency Plans Book

Preface

The easy part of this book was finding the doomsday scenario. The hard part was bringing it to life. I must first acknowledge the assistance I received from the Department of Energy's Nevada office and, most particularly, from Jeff Gordon of the Coordination and Information Center. Over no less than five trips to this archive in North Las Vegas, Jeff patiently helped me obtain photography and textual records that relate to this report.

I must also thank my wife, Jill Johnson Keeney, who read many drafts of this book and in each case helped me work myself out of a hole; and my two sons, Alex and Dougo. In this day and age, computer resources are in demand in every household and for the several weeks of the final draft, I took the lion's share preparing this book.

Of course, I also thank Stephen Schwartz, who for over four years has mentored me in facts nuclear.

The Emergency Plans Book *document was found in the National Archives, Archives II, Silver Springs, Maryland.*

About the Photography

The test firing of a nuclear device is a military and scientific undertaking on the scale of a small war. In some cases, over 10,000 soldiers, sailors, and airmen were required to fire just a handful of bombs. To name just one, aircraft carriers, helicopters from the Marine Corps, destroyers, bombers and fighters of every sort from the Air Force, and countless small watercraft and cargo planes supported Operation Castle, one of the more economical of the many nuclear shots at Pacific Proving Ground in the Marshall Islands. They rigged the test sites, set out the experiments, provided transportation to and from the site, provided security, provided weather reconnaissance flights and weather stations, built barracks, cooked meals, and manned all of the sundry items required to support a mobilized force of this size.

Among these men were camera crews from the Air Force's Lookout Mountain Laboratories in Hollywood, California. Between July 1945 and September 1992, 1,054 nuclear devices were fired. The number of purely atmospheric tests (both aboveground and underwater) between 1946 and 1962 is 166 (66 in the Pacific and 100 in Nevada). Hundreds of thousands—if not more—of still images were made of these explosions and their effects. Sadly, few have been declassified. Those that have been released were not always in good condition. Some were available only as low-resolution digital images (the declassification process began in the post-Internet age). Others are now old prints mounted on warped cardboard and show the signs of aging. Still, they are in most cases the only records anyone has of the explosions, and so they must be used. Accordingly, the quality of the photography in this book may at times appear uneven. For that, little could be done. These are the images as released; in every case the best-quality available was obtained.

All photos are from the author's collection, courtesy of the Department of Energy and/or the Department of Defense.

A view of a 10 megaton thermonuclear blast seen from a distance of 136 miles. This was the Mike shot during Operation Ivy in the South Pacific.

Foreword
By Stephen I. Schwartz

By finding and publishing this work, Doug Keeney has performed an important public service. For although the original *Emergency Plans Book* document, now more than 40 years old, refers to a bygone era, it helps us to understand the motivation of U.S. government officials who spent countless hours—and considerable taxpayer dollars—thinking about ways to cope with the unthinkable. Equally important, this document sheds light on the extraordinary actions of the U.S. government in response to the terrorist attacks on the World Trade Center and the Pentagon on September 11, 2001.

During the Cold War, more than $45 billion was spent to protect both senior U.S. government officials and the general public in the event of a nuclear attack. This funding supported everything from the production and distribution of films and pamphlets instructing citizens how to mitigate the effects of a nuclear blast and fallout to the secret construction of massive underground facilities to allow the government to continue to operate during and after a nuclear war. It is primarily these facilities, and the highly classified plans concerning their use, that were justified by an official doomsday scenario like the one you now hold in your hands.

During the Cold War, ensuring the "continuity of government" was considered of paramount importance. Every president from Harry Truman on has spent considerable time and money preparing for a nuclear war. In addition to the often-visible offensive weaponry that formed the highly visible backbone of our military posture, defensive measures—some public and some secret—were implemented. By the time the plan in this book was written, the United States deployed more than 6,000 nuclear weapons. The Soviet Union, by contrast, had fewer than 700 operational nuclear weapons.

Although it would take another 20 years for the Soviet Union to equal the number of weapons in the U.S. arsenal, the world situation appeared dire in 1958. The *Emergency Plans Book* was distributed about six months after the Soviets launched the first artificial satellite, *Sputnik*, into space. An astonishing technological feat, especially for a country considered by many in the West to be technologically inferior, *Sputnik* alarmed U.S. scientists, policymakers, and military laders alike. They understood that if a rocket could be used to launch a satellite into space, it could also be used to drop nuclear weapons on the United States. Suddenly, we were vulnerable to long-range missile attacks.

Concern about the Soviet Union's ability to destroy or incapacitate the United States began in 1949, following the first Soviet atomic bomb test (a test that surprised military and political leaders but not U.S. scientists, who had correctly predicted shortly after World War II that the Soviet Union was likely to achieve nuclear capability within about four years). This unsettling event was swiftly followed by the Communist revolution in China, the start of the Korean War, revelations of atomic spies (Julius and Ethel Rosenberg and Klaus Fuchs), charges of Communist infiltration of the U.S. government and, in 1953, the first Soviet test of a vastly more powerful hydrogen bomb.

To U.S. leaders at the time, it must have seemed as though World War III was just around the corner.

In response, officials began to prepare for the worst. The *Emergency Plans Book* is one such effort. It matter-of-factly explains what the Soviet Union was capable of doing, what immediate effects a nuclear attack would have on all aspects of U.S. society, and what the longer-term effects were likely to be. That it was kept secret for more than 40 years (and then reclassified shortly after Doug located it at the National Archives in 1998) demonstrates just how sensitive this subject was—and still is.

Even in 1958, officials were pessimistic about the ability of the United States to withstand a nuclear —attack. Nuclear weapons were so immensely destructive that if an attack came, little could be done to mitigate the effects. Eight years before the *Emergency Plans Book* was circulated, a study presented to the National Security Council (NSC) reported that just 16 properly targeted weapons could "most seriously disrupt" government operations. Despite significant expenditures in the years to come, similar findings were reported in the 1960s, 1970s, and 1980s. The fundamental problem was too many weapons and too few highly vulnerable critical targets.

Various measures to protect the public were also considered. But extensive and extremely expensive plans to build massive blast and fallout shelters for the populace were systematically rejected by presidents (who did not want to create a national panic), by Congress (which balked at the price tag), and by military leaders (who argued that it was more sensible and cost effective to invest in offensive weapons to deter war and, if need be, wage war). With the advent of the hydrogen bomb, staying in cities to ride out an attack in a shelter was no longer feasible. As an official who served in the Federal Civil Defense Administration from 1953 to 1957 once explained, the focus shifted from "Duck and Cover" to "Run Like Hell."

Ironically, although the numerous secret Continuity of Government, or CoG, facilities were never fully activated for their intended purpose during the Cold War (nor would they have survived if they had been targeted directly), some of them were put to use on September 11 and afterward. Indeed, in the immediate aftermath of the attacks on the World Trade Center and the Pentagon, the U.S. government implemented emergency plans that until then had been envisioned for use only in the event of an all-out nuclear war.

The most dramatic of these was the decision by the North American Aerospace Defense Command (NORAD) and the Federal Aviation Administration (FAA) to ground all nonmilitary aircraft in U.S. airspace (or in transit to the United States). At 9:25 A.M. Eastern Daylight Time, all aircraft nationwide not already in the air were grounded, and those in the air were ordered to return to where the flight originated or to land at a nearby airport. By 2:07 P.M., all domestic aircraft were on the ground and by 5:30 P.M., all international flights were either on U.S. or Canadian soil. All flights remained grounded until September 13.

The plan under which this order was implemented is known as Security Control of Air Traffic and Navigation Aids, or SCATANA. Developed in the 1960s, SCATANA was originally intended to clear the skies following confirmed warnings of an attack by the Soviet Union. This would have provided unrestricted airspace for U.S. bomber aircraft and missiles, as well as air defense interceptor aircraft, emergency airborne command posts, and associated support aircraft such as refueling tankers. Until September 11, 2001, SCATANA had never been fully implemented, although it was partially activated by accident during a 1979 false alarm at NORAD.

NORAD issued a "notice to airmen" implementing a modified version of SCATANA approximately five hours after American Airlines Flight 11 slammed into the north tower of the World Trade Center. Although all civilian aircraft were grounded, ground navigation aids were not turned off (as they would have been during a nuclear attack), allowing airliners to safely navigate to their new and unexpected destinations.

Also activated in full for the first time on September 11 were the government's CoG plans. Shortly after watching the attacks in New York City on a television in his White House office, Vice President Dick Cheney was evacuated by the Secret Service to the Presidential Emergency Operations Center, a hardened bunker buried beneath the East Wing of the White House. Once there (along with National Security Adviser Condoleeza Rice, Transportation Secretary Norman Mineta, and a few other staff members), Cheney used a secure telephone to contact President George W. Bush, who was in Sarasota, Florida, visiting an elementary school. As Cheney told NBC's *Meet the Press* on September 16, in his conversation with the president he "strongly urge[d] him to delay his return" because of fears that Washington, D.C., was going to be attacked (fears compounded by a telephone call to the Secret Service indicating—erroneously as it turned out—that Air Force One was an intended target).

Bush subsequently boarded Air Force One and took to the air as officials scrambled to ascertain what was happening. At one point, the Secret Service considered sending him to NORAD's headquarters inside Cheyenne Mountain near Colorado Springs, Colorado. After touching down for almost two hours at Barksdale Air Force Base near Bossier City, Louisiana (site of the U.S. Strategic Command's (Stratcom) alternate underground command post) to deliver a hastily prepared statement, the president headed to Offutt Air Force Base near Omaha, Nebraska, communicating with Cheney, military leaders, and the National Security Council via secure teleconference and videoconference links from Stratcom's primary underground command post, before eventually returning to Washington, D.C., in the evening.

On September 11, U.S. forces worldwide were placed on Defense Condition (DefCon) 3, a heightened state of alert that also entails readying forces for war (with DefCon 5 signifying peacetime and DefCon 1 denoting maximum readiness for combat), and possibly at DefCon 2. It is therefore probable that the military's fleet of airborne command posts, including the ones based at Omaha (nicknamed "Looking Glass") were placed under increased security and that preparations were made to make them airborne. It is also likely that the president's specially shielded and outfitted airborne command post, known as the National Airborne Operations Center, or NAOC (code-named "Night Watch"), was readied (it is normally kept on 15-minute ground alert). Indeed, the president's diversion to Omaha suggests that officials were at least contemplating moving him from Air Force One to NAOC where he could, if necessary, remain aloft for as long as 72 hours while directing a military response.

From the White House bunker, Cheney ordered the evacuation of everyone designated by law as a successor to the president, including the Speaker of the House of Representatives, Representative Dennis Hastert, Republican of Illinois; the president pro tempore of the Senate, Robert C. Byrd, Democrat of West Virginia; and the entire Cabinet (except Defense Secretary Donald Rumsfeld, who remained at the Pentagon), as well the rest of the congressional leadership (the remaining members of Congress were merely instructed to leave their Capitol Hill offices). The Secret Service tried at least twice to convince Cheney to evacuate as well, "but I didn't want to leave the node that we'd established there in terms of having all this capability tied together by communications—and if I'd left, all of that would have been broken down—so I thought it was appropriate for me to stay there in the White House."

Hastert, and presumably most if not all the others who were in the Washington, D.C., area, were picked up at designated assembly points by Marine Corps helicopters kept ready for that purpose and transported to "a secure facility," most likely the Federal Emergency Management Agency's (FEMA) bunker known as the High Point Special Facility, or simply "SF," inside Mount Weather near Berryville, Virginia, 48 miles (approximately 20 minutes) by air from Washington. (Senior officials who happened to be away from Washington would have been taken to one or more of the many emergency relocation sites situated throughout the country. According to a former official from the White House Military Office, by 1980 there were reportedly more than 75 such facilities.) The underground complex at Mount Weather, which was built over four years at a cost of more than $1 billion and opened in 1958, contains an estimated 600,000 square feet of floor space. The facility, which was designed to accommodate several thousand people, includes a hospital, dining and recreation areas, sleeping quarters, an emergency power plant, a radio and television studio, a direct link to the White House, storage tanks capable of holding 500,000 gallons of water, and a crematorium. The only previous time High Point was fully activated was November 9, 1965, during a major power blackout across much of the northeast United States.

Until 1995, most members of Congress and selected staff members would have been taken to a secret bunker (code-named "Casper" and later "Greek Island") 64 feet beneath the prestigious Greenbrier resort in White Sulphur Springs, West Virginia. This 112,000-square-foot facility included a complete medical clinic, television studio, decontamination showers, and a "pathological waste incinerator." The facility, which could accommodate about 1,000 people for two months and was sealed off with 20-ton blast doors, included separate chambers for the House of Representatives and the Senate, as well as a larger room for joint sessions. After its existence was revealed in an article in the *Washington Post Magazine* in 1992, the site was decommissioned in 1995 and opened to the public for tours in 1996.

Alternatively, some of the officials evacuated on September 11 may have been sent to Site R, officially known as the Alternate Joint Communications Center. Since 1953, Site R has served as the backup Pentagon, with more than 700,000 square feet of floor space, so-phisticated computer and communications equipment, a reservoir, chapel, and room for more than 3,000 peo-ple. Located inside Raven Rock Mountain about 6 miles north of Camp David on the Pennsylvania-Mary-land border, Site R continued to operate as a major CoG facility even as other facilities were mothballed in the 1990s. As recently as 1997, it had more than 500 mil-itary and civilian personnel reportedly working there (although not on round-the-clock shifts, which ended in February 1992).

During the Cold War, every federal agency had its own emergency relocation site for use during and after a nuclear war. These were arrayed in an arc around Washington, D.C., far enough from the city, it was hoped, to avoid immediate destruction, yet close enough to allow relocating officials to reach the sites in time. Senior officials at the Treasury De-partment worked from their relocation site on Septem-ber 11, as did officials from the Nuclear Regulatory Commission; it is likely that officials from other de-partments did as well. *U.S. News and World Report* subsequently reported that nearly two months later, emergency teams from most government agencies continued to work out of their relocation bunkers. Had the events of September 11 involved something more destructive than four hijacked airplanes, addi-tional emergency plans may have been imple-mented. For decades (and perhaps even today), the U.S. Postal Service has had regulations on the books detailing how to handle and decontaminate mail, distribute change-of-address cards for survivors of a nuclear war, and burn stamps to prevent their "falling into enemy hands." For its part, the Internal

Revenue Service (IRS) held regular exercises on how to assess and collect taxes following a nuclear attack.

Fear and uncertainty about the terrorists' plans, the whereabouts of any accomplices, and ongoing concerns about the safety of the president in Washington, D.C., led Vice President Cheney to spend his evenings and perhaps some days of the remainder of that week at the presidential retreat at Camp David, where there is also a secure, if rather austere, underground shelter. At least one television report suggested Cheney was also spending time at Site R during this tense period, a wholly plausible scenario. As late as September 20, when President Bush ventured to Capitol Hill to address the nation, security concerns kept Cheney away, reportedly the first time a vice president has not appeared with a president before a joint session of Congress (Senator Byrd took his seat on the dais). House majority leader Richard Armey, Republican of Texas, also skipped the event at the request of security officials.

Even nearly a month later, the vice president was still spending a significant amount of time at an "undisclosed location." In an interview with Jim Lehrer on the Public Broadcasting System on October 12, Cheney, who had just returned to Washington after four days at a secret site, explained that "we've reached the point where, especially with Washington targeted as it was on September 11, that generally it's not a good practice for the president and I [sic] to spend a lot of time together." Although Cheney did not divulge where he had been spending time, he did acknowledge that, "we have secure facilities that have been developed over the years for good and sufficient reasons; they come in handy now at a time like this."

How well all of this worked is as yet unknown and is, in any event, highly classified.

While there are still regular emergency evacuation drills for designated senior officials, and although the White House Communications Agency and FEMA still track the location of each duly designated presidential successor, there were almost certainly a few problems locating everyone and getting all of the equipment and communications links up and running.

Would any of this have worked in the scenario envisioned in the *Emergency Plans Book*? The stark and realistic answer is no. "Governmental control is seriously jeopardized and central Federal direction is virtually non-existent," say the documents. "Washington was so severely damaged that no operations there are possible. . . . Because of heavy fallout, none of the personnel at a few of the relocation sites survived . . . the social fabric has ceased to exist. . . . Confusion is widespread . . . and customary control and direction are non-existent."

Bud Gallagher, the director of Mount Weather from 1967 to 1992, put it well in an interview with *Time* magazine. "Through the years, we always reacted like we could handle an all-out nuclear attack. I don't think people—even our top people in government—have any idea of what a thousand multi-megaton nuclear weapons on the U.S. would do. We'd be back in the Stone Age. It's unthinkable." President Eisenhower had no illusions about the magnitude of the problem. He told his Cabinet in 1956, "Government which goes on with some kind of continuity will be like a one-eyed man in the land of the blind."

While the CoG plans apparently worked well on September 11, the evacuations of all federal government buildings and many private office buildings in New York City; Washington, D.C.; Chicago; and elsewhere created massive traffic jams, bringing traffic in some areas to a standstill for hours. This demonstrated once and for all the utter unreality and futility of all the civil defense plans devised by government officials, who from the 1950s through the 1980s promoted orderly citywide evacuations to the countryside as the best means of defense against a nuclear attack. Now more than ever, it is clear that there can be no effective defense against a large-scale nuclear attack.

Nevertheless, some measure of comfort can be taken from the fact that facilities that had seemed irrelevant have become useful again in our fight against terror. And yet it is still appropriate to ask: With so much attention, and money, devoted to safeguarding government leaders and so little to protecting the public, would there be anyone or anything left to govern in the event of a truly catastrophic large-scale attack upon the United States?

Stephen I. Schwartz is publisher of the *Bulletin of the Atomic Scientists* and the editor and co-author of *Atomic Audit: The Costs and Consequences of U.S. Nuclear Weapons Since 1940* (Brookings Institution Press, 1998).

Operation Hardtack. This is how a port would look during the initial wave of an attack. An underwater nuclear depth charge has exploded and silhouettes a drone convoy ship. The plumes from underwater explosions are powerful indeed. It was not uncommon for water to skyrocket one mile high in less than a second.

Introduction

Nevil Shute's 1957 classic, *On the Beach,* is a haunting story about the end of the world. The setting is post–World War III. A horrific exchange of nuclear weapons has wiped out the Northern Hemisphere and a belt of radiation is now descending over the southern latitudes, slowly extinguishing life as it goes. A U.S. submarine has reached Australia and has sought refuge there but, as the end nears, the crew departs for a final survey of their homeland. The submarine traverses the oceans and reaches the West Coast of the United States. In one of the final chapters, the captain brings his ship to a halt offshore a small fishing town. He raises the periscope. Although the streets are ghostly empty, lights still shine in the windows of the homes and a radio transmits a sporadic signal. This small town, not in the least damaged by the bombs but shrouded in contamination, reeks of innocence lost. As with the rest of America, everyone is dead.

At the height of the Cold War, a fear gripped America that I remember well, even though at the time, I was just a child. It was the feeling of being held hostage to a fate that one was helpless to do much about. It was the fear of a surprise nuclear attack on the United States by the Soviets. A surprise attack in and of itself was not terribly alarming. Surprise is the nature of war. The hard part to swallow was the use of nuclear weapons. If they were used, and all presumed that that they would be, there was little chance the average family would survive. Succinctly reducing this to a single sentence was a report issued by the Manhattan Project on the eve of the first atomic bomb test. It said, with grave profundity: "In no other type of warfare does the advantage lie so heavily with the aggressor."

To keep aggression at bay, the high-wire act of the Cold War was to convince the other side that even in the face of a nuclear attack, a retaliatory force sufficient to destroy them could survive the very worst. This concept was called Mutually Assured Destruction (MAD). The key to MAD was to be certain that we survived. So important was this that the entire readiness posture of the Strategic Air Command (SAC), and of our ground forces in Europe through 1989, was oriented to that end.

That America had a doomsday scenario is well known, but no copy has ever been released. Instead, portraying the attack that ends the world has largely been left to the imagination of moviemakers—and to such authors as Shute. Late in the summer of 1998, however, the National Archives in Washington, D.C., announced the declassification of a Record Group that contained the formerly "Secret" files from the Office of the Secretary of the Air Force. As an author who frequently used the considerable assets of the Archives, the announcement was reason to be excited. New Record Groups often open doors to new understandings of historically important events and this one, which centered around one of the most secret of military eras, the Cold War years, had the earmarking of all that and more.

That in mind, I flew to College Park, Maryland, where the Still Media Records of the Archives are located, and settled in for several days of research. I requested files beginning in 1956 and patiently thumbed through reams of original letters, reports, and memorandums, all of them at one time stamped classified. On my third day, I came upon a folder titled *The Emergency Plans Book*. It was stamped "Secret" and was written by the Assistant Secretary of Defense for Emergency Planning. It was dated

1958. The *Emergency Plans Book*, said the foreword, was the "latest and only approved guidance to the department and agencies" for defense mobilization planning in the event of "a direct attack on the [United States]." Continuing, it said that it had been "authorized by the National Security Council." Those receiving a copy represented the nation's highest judicial and military offices, including the Director of the National Security Agency, the Chairman of the Joint Chiefs of Staff, the General Counsel for the United States, and the Secretaries of the Army, Air Force, and Navy.

As I read this document I realized that, despite this rather dry name, *The Emergency Plans Book* was in fact the elusive doomsday scenario. My heart rate quickened. I immediately requested a declassification sticker, affixed it to the plate of a copy machine and ran off a complete photocopy. Good thing I did. When I returned to the Archives in 1999, the entire Record Group had been removed. Said an archivist familiar with the circumstances, a "high-ranking Air Force colonel" had read some of the materials and immediately had it reclassified secret. This remarkable document once again resides in the Silver Springs facility on the eighth floor, a floor reserved only for those with Top Secret clearances. The doomsday scenario is again classified. Except this copy.

The *Emergency Plans Book* is a military scenario. It describes a nuclear attack on America by Soviet air, navy, and ballistic forces and parses no detail in describing the destruction that would ensue. Despite the Nike-Ajax missile batteries that were then positioned around our major cities, and even considering our much flaunted air interceptor fighter squadrons that were based along the nation's perimeter, the doomsday scenario says that a sizeable enemy force would penetrate our defenses, reach their targets, and release their bombs. Kiloton- and megaton-sized weapons would pummel our industrial, transportation, communication, and financial centers in a sustained downpouring of warheads. The national landscape would be blurred with smoke and haze and littered with death and destruction and contamination, with only the most rudimentary fragments of community and government surviving. Said the *Emergency Plans Book*, "12,500,000 are suffering from blast or thermal injuries and have an immediate and evident need for treatment." The surviving labor force is "engaged in large numbers in disposing of the dead." Our shipping ports are clogged with sunken ships; we would be a nation of people scrounging for food, with crematoriums working around the clock.

We do strike back. According to the scenario, our forces are engaging the enemy on all fronts. Still, the nuclear exchange described herein is all but the end of the world.

As with any military documents, words are utterly important and their meaning should be understood. For example, saying that a nuclear bomb was a "megaton" weapon (versus a smaller "kiloton" weapon) suggests that the Soviets would use a sophisticated bomb that was not yet in our own national stockpiles (our thermonuclear weapons were thought to be five years ahead of anything the Soviets had developed yet the scenario suggests otherwise). Profound, too, is the carefully worded section on the Soviet preemplacement of atomic weapons within the United States by "clandestine" means, a chilling admission that even in

1958 the Pentagon foresaw the activation of "sleeper" agents or some other means of infiltration.

Thankfully, the *Emergency Plans Book* was not where federal readiness ended. To the contrary, what emanated from them was something called Continuity of Government (CoG) plans. The origins of CoG go back to the Truman administration. In the late 1950s, and through the early 1970s, a decapitating attack on America was presumed to be a nuclear attack and because of that, survivability of a functioning federal government was doubtful, but not impossible. The key was to be prepared—prepared with succession plans, and with survival shelters. Thus, between 1958 and through the present, tens of billions of dollars were spent to build perhaps hundreds of CoG shelters, safe houses, and relocation bunkers. Some of the bunkers were deep inside mountains; others were below the very buildings most likely to be targeted first. The White House, for instance, has beneath it a bombproof fallout shelter and nearby, a garage holding the excavation machinery necessary to dig the president out.

Lest they aid the enemy, CoG remains one of the nation's most guarded secrets. That said, some information is known. It is known, for instance, that there were (and are) specific CoG plans that separately spell out how the president, vice president, and key members of the cabinet, along with essential federal agencies, should evacuate their offices, and how they'd be transported to facilities presumed to be safe from continued aggression. Here they would reestablish operations. Other plans addressed the seemingly inocuous, such as how the U.S. Postal Service would readdress streets that no longer exist, and the ponderous—where should the Federal Reserve could keep a reserve of fresh currency?The important point, is this: CoG plans emanate from the doomsday scenario. They are designed to preserve the government in the aftermath.

Could CoG plans achieve their ends? As you read in the foreword, most historians think not. The thermonuclear bomb was such a powerful and versatile weapon that, even in 1958, it was assumed that many of the relocation centers would be destroyed. CoG was activated during the Cuban Missile Crisis in 1962 but the crisis never escalated to a confrontation. Thankfully, America was never attacked, not during the Cold War. But years later, when a lesser but nonetheless potentially decapitating attack did occur, these same plans came to the fore.

September 11, 2001

On September 11, 2001, the doomsday scenario came suddenly to life. Forces presumed to be affiliated with Osama bin Laden unleashed a no-notice attack on federal and civilian targets. Terrorists hijacked and crashed fully fueled Boeing 757 and 767 airliners into the sides of the twin towers of the World Trade Center, and into the Pentagon. Although they had little notice, a C-130 made a visual ID while the Weapons Desk at NORAD Sector Control at Tyndall Air Force Base (AFB) in Panama City, Florida, scrambled F-15 and F-16 fighter interceptors from Langley AFB, Virginia, and Otis AFB on Cape Cod. The jets were launched and airborne and although they streaked through the sky at Mach 1.5, there wasn't enough time to stop the attacks. Clouds of smoke rose above Washington, D.C., and New York City. A fourth airplane crashed in Pennsylvania. There was a report of a fifth plane. A period of confusion ensued. Were more attacks imminent? The destruction had all the earmarkings of the doomsday scenario, and so no one could take the chance. While Americans sat before their television sets, stunned by what they saw, CoG plans were activated. The president was hurried to Air Force One and was quickly airborne. Air Force One first flew up the coast from Miami to Jacksonville, but then in keeping with CoG diverted to Barksdale Air Force Base for a brief stop and then continued to Offutt AFB, Nebraska, where a Cold War CoG facility was operational. In an interesting twist of symmetry, this facility was at the former headquarters of the Strategic Air Command, the force that in the Cold War was responsible for mounting the retaliatory strike. It was here that the president bunkered for several hours.

Back in Washington, D.C., other CoG plans were activated. The Speaker of the House, the president pro tempore of the Senate, and key officials were whisked off to secure locations. The Central Locator System was likely activated. Members of the Federal Reserve, each of the cabinets—all of the vital government offices—went to the bunkers, literally and figuratively. The president was not to be seen by the public for hours; so, too, the vice president. In the weeks following, President Bush would several times acknowledge that rarely was he in the same building as the vice president who, as the press often reported, was in a "secure undisclosed location." The president acknowledged that this was in keeping with extant CoG planning.

The *Emergency Plans Book* was the cornerstone for emergency preparedness; CoG plans were the cornerstone for survivability. Reacting just as they would had this been a nuclear attack, key government officials were secreted in their designated Cold War shelters. They could no longer be targeted. They were safe. Democracy was preserved. Thus it was that this Cold War doomsday scenario, and those like it handed down for one president to another, suddenly became relevant—and on September 11 we saw the benefits firsthand.

Understanding the Plans

Since acquiring my copy of *Emergency Plans Book* I have done little with it. However, as one of the few researchers to even access the Secretary of Air Force files (their release was not broadly announced), I suspected that I might be the only person to have it. I decided to share a copy with a few friends and fellow authors. Not surprisingly, they encouraged me to publish it. Again, I hesitated. I felt the *Emergency Plans Book* was too short to sustain a conventional press run but too important to be shouldered in between advertisements for underwear in a glossy magazine. If it were to be published, I wanted it to stand on its own, to be read as I had read it, to be seen starkly unadorned. But I wasn't sure how to make that happen.

The answer came from my wife, who is a journalist of considerable talent, and from Stephen Schwartz, who writes the foreword to this book. Steve, publisher of the *Bulletin of the Atomic Scientists*, is perhaps one of the most knowledgeable nuclear history experts in the nation. Not only did he receive resounding accolades for his 680-page book published in 1998, *Atomic Audit,* but he chaired the Nuclear Weapons Cost Study Project at the Brookings Institution. My wife and Steve helped me see the tie between *Plans*, CoG and the events of September 11th.

There was a loose end to tie up, too. When this was declassified in 1998, a section called Military Effects was held back, presumably for reasons of national security. This missing section, I feel certain, would have explained and documented the size and yields of different warheads, as well as their capabilities based on fusing, be it a land burst, an airburst, an underwater burst, and so on. The military effects of nuclear weapons have, however, been released through other outlets, most notably, through the Department of Energy (DOE). Under Secretary of Energy Hazel O'Leary, the DOE launched an Openness Initiative. Under this initiative, literally millions of pages of documents, and hundreds of photographs, were made public. Many of these document the weapons effects as experienced at the Nevada Test Site, north of Las Vegas, and the Pacific Proving Grounds, in the Marshall Islands.

Through these photos, I began to visualize the battles portrayed in the *Emergency Plans Book.* I could see the blast effects of a thermonuclear bomb on homes, factories, and military material; I could understand the thermal pulse, the underwater shock wave, and the other nuclear effects that, according to the *Emergency Plans Book,* would so thoroughly ravage our nation. I have included selections of photos from the DOE archives. I think they add immeasurably to the understanding of the *Emergency Plans Book*, and, in many ways, fill in for the missing section.

Some comments on the material are appropriate. First, in preparing this for publication, I resisted the temptation to edit anything. The original author has taken into consideration the considerable Soviet military capabilities, the training of their pilots, the readiness of the SAC (which was then on 15-minute ground alerts), the effectiveness of our countermeasures, the vulnerabilities of our cities and military bases and relocation centers to an attack, and portrays the results. He speaks of the loss of our forests, the regionalization of our economies, the extreme medical crisis, a period of intense radiation, and the horrid conditions for those who survive for the reconstruction period. I found the voice and the structure of the original document to be utterly compelling in its original form. Thus, I edited nothing of the actual doomsday text. It is not sensational or exploitative but rather matter-of-fact. This is how insiders saw it. You will read it as it was written.

I have, however, added contextual notes. They provide, I feel, necessary clarification and, in some cases, amplify points that might otherwise be lost to the stark wording and crisp pacing of the text.

Finally, I have added some definitions. The *Emergency Plans Book* was sent to some rather remarkable people—cabinet members, intelligence agencies, and all of the military branches—however, you may not know the meaning of one of the offices. "The Armed Forces Special Weapons Project" is a multibranch, military oversight group that controlled the use of nuclear weapons by the four nuclearized forces: the Army, the Air Force, the Navy, and the Marines (the Coast Guard was never nuclearized).

"Special Weapons" is another term unique to the military. Nuclear bombs, nuclear missiles, nuclear torpedoes, air-to-air missiles, and artillery shells—anything that has been nuclearized—are "special weapons," a name, presumably, indicating that the weapons will be used in only the most special of circumstances—dire ones, no doubt.

There is another term that may be confusing. That word is CONUS. CONUS stands for <u>CON</u>tinental <u>U</u>nited <u>S</u>tates

Armageddon in Perspective: 1958 to Today

The emergency plans in this book were approved in 1958, but we do know that at least six presidents since Truman have built on this scenario, adjusting it, and their CoG plans, in accordance with the evolving threat. Documents show that Presidents Eisenhower, Kennedy, Reagan, Carter, Clinton, and George Bush each oversaw major Emergency War Plans initiatives and created or modified the missions of agencies responsible for the nation's CoG plans. To name but two, the National Security Resources Board (1947 to 1953) was the first agency charged with emergency preparedness; the Federal Emergency Management Agency (1978 to present) fills that role today.

No matter the name, each agency had a common goal. Said Executive Order 12656, the agencies were to ensure "the continuity of essential [federal] functions in any national security emergency by providing for succession to office and emergency delegation of authority in accordance with applicable law; safekeeping of essential resources, facilities, and records; and establishment of emergency operating facilities." True in the Cold War. True in the cold light of terrorism.

Without doubt, this is a somber document. Thankfully, the military did not succumb to temptation and sugarcoat scenarios such as these. While the public perception during the Cold War may have been naive—that World War III could be survived with little more than "an underground shelter with 3 feet of dirt above it," as one civil defense brochure put it—privately, Washington was thinking something different indeed. Privately, they were pouring tens of billions of dollars into shelters for a post–World War III America.

This is not science fiction. This is how America might have ended. It is also how a Cold War scenario became so useful in the face of cold-blooded terrorism.

The chapel at Camp Desert Rock, Nevada. Part of the compound at the Nevada Test Site, soldiers and marines were billeted at Desert Rock before going down to the trenches around ground zero for nuclear indoctrination. Over 500 semi-permanent buildings and 600 tents made up the Camp. Desert Rock exercises were held between 1951 and 1955. *Nevada Test Site*

The Official United States Government Doomsday Scenario

SECRET

OFFICE OF THE ASSISTANT SECRETARY OF DEFENSE
WASHINGTON 25, D. C.

23 April 1958

MANPOWER, PERSONNEL AND RESERVE

MEMORANDUM FOR THE SECRETARIES OF THE MILITARY DEPARTMENTS
           THE ASSISTANT SECRETARIES OF DEFENSE
           THE GENERAL COUNSEL
           THE ASSISTANTS TO THE SECRETARY OF DEFENSE
           THE DIRECTOR, GUIDED MISSILES
           THE DIRECTOR, ADVANCED RESEARCH PROJECTS AGENCY
           THE CHAIRMAN, JOINT CHIEFS OF STAFF
           THE CHIEF, ARMED FORCES SPECIAL WEAPONS PROJECT
                AND
           THE DIRECTOR, NATIONAL SECURITY AGENCY

SUBJECT: Revision of Emergency Plans Book

    It is intended that the Emergency Plans Book (EPB) of the Department of Defense will be brought up to date as of 1 June 1958.

    Addressees are requested: (a) to review sections of the Emergency Plans Book which pertain to emergency plans and actions over which they have cognizance; and (b) to submit on or before 23 May 1958, either an indication that no changes are necessary, or changes which are to be included in the proposed revision of the EPB.

    The situation assumptions, planning information, actions, operational assignments and organization, and appendices, in Mobilization Plan C, approved 1 June 1957 for planning policy and guidance, will be used for purposes of reviewing Department of Defense plans and actions for the situations resulting from enemy attack on U.S. Forces outside the CONUS.

    Attached for use in reviewing DOD emergency plans and actions to be implemented in the event of a direct attack on CONUS, is a copy of "Capabilities Assumptions" (Part I-A, pp. 1-2), the "Situation Assumptions -- The Attack" (Part I-C, pp. 27-29), and the "Situation Assumptions -- Post Attack Analysis" (Part I-C, pp. 30-43) of ODM Mobilization Plan D-Minus. These sections were noted by the NSC, at its 11 July 1957 meeting, as being suitable for defense mobilization planning for a surprise attack on the CONUS. They constitute the latest and only approved guidance to the departments and agencies on the D-Minus type situations.

J. W. Oien
Acting Director
Office of Emergency Planning

Incl.
As stated
DS 58-4333-A₁

SECRET 61631 1434-58

CP-S-58-342

DECLASSIFIED
Authority NND 789005
By DCO NARA Date 8/5/98

35

MEMORANDUM FOR:

THE SECRETARIES OF THE MILITARY
  DEPARTMENTS
THE ASSISTANT SECRETARIES OF DEFENSE
THE GENERAL COUNSEL
THE ASSISTANTS TO THE SECRETARY
  OF DEFENSE
THE DIRECTOR, GUIDED MISSILES
THE CHAIRMAN, JOINT CHIEFS OF STAFF
THE CHIEF, ARMED FORCES SPECIAL
  WEAPONS PROJECT AND THE DIRECTOR,
  NATIONAL SECURITY AGENCY

FROM: J.W. CLEAR
OFFICE OF EMERGENCY PLANNING
ACTING DIRECTOR

23 APRIL 1958

SECRET

SUBJECT: Revision of *Emergency Plans Book*

See note #1

1. This particular copy of the *Emergency Plans Book* is the copy sent to Secretary of the Air Force James H. Douglas Jr., 1957–1959. It is authored by the Office of Emergency Planning, the Department of Defense, which can be traced directly to today's FEMA. Here's the lineage. The Federal Civil Defense Administration (FCDA) was established in the Office for Emergency Management by Executive Order 10186 of December 1, 1950, and was subsequently established as an independent agency by act of Congress on January 12, 1951. It operated between 1951 and 1958, when this document was written. Just months after this document, its functions were transferred to the Office of Defense and Civil Mobilization (ODCM). In 1961, the OCDM was abolished. Most of its functions were transferred to the Defense Civil Preparedness Agency of the Department of Defense before being transferred to the Federal Emergency Management Agency in 1979 by President Jimmy Carter. FEMA, as with its predecessors, administers the national civil defense program, and coordinates military, industrial, and civilian mobilization in the event of emergencies.

FEMA, which today seems to be more of a natural-disaster relief agency, was and is responsible for nuclear readiness, as well as the survival of the federal government after a nuclear, biological, or chemical attack. This role diminished (at least in the eye of the public) after the breakup of the Soviet Union, but it today remains a clearly stated mission of FEMA. According to Executive Order 12148, which established FEMA, FEMA would be responsible for any civil emergency, a term that was clearly defined. Said 12148: "A 'civil emergency' means any accidental, natural, man-caused, or wartime emergency or threat thereof, which causes or may cause substantial injury or harm to the population or substantial damage to or loss of property." FEMA is an independent agency reporting to the president but, because of its wartime (or terrorism) component, it has DOD oversight in some areas. Again, according to Executive Order 12148 : "In order that civil defense planning continues to be fully compatible with the Nation's overall strategic policy, and in order to maintain an effective link between strategic nuclear planning and nuclear attack preparedness planning, the development of civil defense policies and programs by the Director of the Federal Emergency Management Agency shall be subject to oversight by the Secretary of Defense and the National Security Council."

It is intended that the *Emergency Plan Book* (EPB) of the Department of Defense will be brought up to date as of 1 June 1958.

Addressees are requested: (a) to review sections of the Plan Book which pertain to emergency plans and actions over which they have cognizance; and (b) to submit on or before 23 May 1958, either an indication that no plans are necessary, or changes which are to be included in the proposed revision of the EPB.

The situation assumptions, planning information, actions, operational assignments and organization, and appendices, in Mobilization Plan C, approved 1 June 1957 for planning policy and guidance, will be used for purposes of reviewing Department of Defense plans and actions for the situations resulting from enemy attack on U.S. Forces outside the CONUS.

See note #2, #3, and #4

2. Since the passage in 1947 of the National Security Act, the federal government has actively promulgated national civil defense programs. These include industrial and civilian mobilization programs; continuity of government operations; cultural preservation programs; emergency planning for nuclear, biological, and conventional attack; terrorism; fallout shelters; and a national warning system. All of these emanate from the doomsday scenarios. Doomsday scenarios were worst-case, but nonetheless probable, scenarios. Mobilization programs were held up against them to pass the test of reasonableness: Should this scenario come about, can we continue government? Are we prepared?

In 1962, President John F. Kennedy asked for a ground-up review of his CoG plans. Said McGeorge Bundy in National Security Action Memorandum No. 127, 1962, the study should include "an examination of the present relocation plans for Federal personnel, including the procedures for selecting the necessary emergency personnel, the physical relocation sites and their communications, and the evacuation plans for moving personnel to the relocation centers." The memo goes on to add that the Committee should place particular emphasis "on the plans for insuring the survival of the Presidency."

A number of names have been pinned to these programs. President Jimmy Carter called them Continuity of Government but the Reagan administration tossed in a new one: "Enduring National Leadership." The Bush administration came up with their own moniker, "Enduring Constitutional Government" while in 1990, President William Clinton issued Presidential Decision Directive 67 asking all federal agencies to prepare Continuity of Operations Plans for Essential Operations under his Enduring Constitutional Government program. Owing to the reduced threat from the former Soviet Union, Clinton's ECG initiatives significantly scaled back CoG programs and funding.

Attached for use in reviewing DOD emergency plans and actions to be implemented in the event of a direct attack on CONUS, is a copy of "Capability Assumptions" (Part I-A, pp.1-2), the "Situation Assumptions–The Attack" (Part I-C, pp. 27-29), and the "Situation Assumptions–Post Attack Analysis" (Part I-C, pp. 30-43) of ODM Mobilization Plan D-Minus. These sections were noted by the NSC, at its 11 July 1957 meeting, as being suitable for defense mobilization planning for a surprise attack on the CONUS. They constitute the latest and only approved guidance to the departments and agencies on the D-Minus type situations.

3. There were three sections to the *Plans* document, named Part I-A, Part I-B, and Part I-C. Two of these sections, I-A and I-C, were declassified; Part I-B, was not. Part I-B is later identified as "Weapons Effects" (see page **50**). The term "weapons effects" is a military term that makes comfortable its true meaning. "Weapons effects" simply means "damage and destruction." A nuclear bomb—using the word "nuclear" loosely; a true nuclear bomb is a fusion bomb while an atomic bomb is a smaller, fission bomb—has three "effects." These are blast, thermal, and radiation effects. As a general rule, a nuclear bomb's blast effects are the most destructive. The fast-released overpressure of a nuke's shock wave slams into structures like a freight train. The thermal pulse—the heat wave generated by a bomb—can vaporize or burn almost anything within a mile or two of ground zero. Radiation is hard to quantify. Radiation effects have more to do with the height above ground a bomb explodes. A ground burst or an underwater burst is the dirtiest explosion and would heavily contaminate ground zero. An airburst leaves ground zero relatively "clean" because the bomb sucks upward into the fireball the ground debris that is then ionized and blows downwind. This 25-page section presumably detailed the destructive capabilities of different types of bombs. These data would be based on the effects tests conducted at either the Nevada Test Site or the Pacific Proving Grounds. Over 1,000 atomic or nuclear bombs were exploded at these sites.

4. The importance of this document is revealed in the last paragraph of this cover note. Here we see that the doomsday scenario is the foundation for the plans other agencies must prepare. Says the author, the *Emergency Plans Book* has been reviewed by the National Security Council, which has declared it "suitable for defense mobilization planning" in the event of a surprise attack. Moreover, the author asserts that this document "constitute[s] the latest and only approved guidance to the departments and agencies" on the nature of a surprise attack by the Soviets. As such, it should be used for "reviewing DOD emergency plans and actions to be implemented in the event of a direct attack on CONUS."

**PLAN
D-MINUS
MAY 1, 1957**

PART I. PLANNING INFORMATION

A. CAPABILITY ASSUMPTIONS*

CAPABILITY ASSUMPTIONS are statements of assumed capabilities of the USSR, known effects of atomic weapons and assumed advanced warning capabilities of our own forces. CAPABILITY ASSUMPTIONS are not statements of intent nor of what the USSR will do. They are statements designed to give uniform interpretation to the knowledge of various agencies engaged in defense mobilization planning. All CAPABILITY ASSUMPTIONS, as well as all other assumptions in Part I–Planning Information, are consistent with intelligence sources. It is within the range and scope of the CAPABILITY ASSUMPTIONS that SITUATION ASSUMPTIONS and POLICY ASSUMPTIONS have been developed.

See note #5 and #6

42

5. The author makes it crystal clear that the capability assumptions in this document are based on the international intelligence-gathering assets of our country and as such, they were ironclad. Where did we get such data? One of the lesser-known aspects of the Cold War was that the U.S. Air Force and Navy routinely conducted overflights of Soviet territory to intercept electronic signals. Unheard of today (and not only because of satellites; such intrusions would be reason enough to start a war), some of these flights went inland as much as 200 miles or more; many triggered air-to-air combat; some of our planes were shot down. But it was the U-2 that was by now providing the very best firsthand intelligence data on Soviet military capabilities. By 1956, the Central Intelligence Agency (CIA) was sending the U-2 on missions that brazenly crisscrossed the entire face of the Soviet Union. The first overflight occurred on July 4, 1956. The pilot flew over Minsk, Belorussia, and Leningrad, freely snapping photos on a camera built by Edwin H. Land, the founder of Polaroid. On this flight, over a dozen attempts were made to shoot the U-2 down but, to the chagrin of the Soviets, it flew too high and too fast to be reached by surface-to-air missiles or their fighters.

6. D-Minus. The key assumption made in the *Emergency Plans Book* document was that the Soviets would launch a full-scale attack against the United States. The date of the attack will be called D-Day and the outcomes will be measured in time intervals from D-Day forward. The document begins on D-Minus—the days before the attack. At this pre-attack starting point, the author summarizes what intelligence agencies believed to be true Soviet offensive capabilities and incorporates the relative effectiveness of American defensive countermeasures.

1. The USSR is capable of:

a. Producing atomic weapons of varying yields ranging from a few kilotons (thousands of tons) to megatons (millions of tons) of TNT equivalent, biological and chemical agents, and incendiary and high-explosive weapons.

b. Delivering these weapons anywhere within the United States and upon U.S.-deployed forces and Allies by piloted aircraft, submarine-launched missiles or mines or clandestine means.

c. Fusing these weapons for air or surface burst or for delayed action.

d. Employing propaganda, psychological warfare, and sabotage.

e. Supporting a large-scale war effort.

See note #7, #8, #9, and #10

7. The United States successfully tested a deliverable megaton bomb only four years prior to the writing of this plan (Operation Castle). The first production megaton weapon was, in 1958, just then being received in the U.S. nuclear stockpiles (the Mark 15, a 1.4-megaton design). The planners here assume that the Soviets were at least on par with our own stockpiles, if not ahead.

8. It is important to see the link between 1958 and today. Biological and chemical weapons have been part of military arsenals since mustard gas was used during World War I. Our own research into these weapons was extensive. The Army was actively refining biological and chemical warfare at its Dugway Proving Grounds near Salt Lake City. Even in 1958, it was assumed that America would be attacked by biological and chemical weapons, a scenario no different from the anthrax cases that followed the terrorist attacks of September 11, 2001.

9. The ability to deliver weapons "anywhere in the United States" is another carefully thought-out assumption. It acknowledges that the Soviets had superb aeronautical design and manufacturing capabilities. An example of this was the Soviet Tupolev Tu-95 Bear A which was routinely spotted flying up and down our East Coast. It had a 9,000-mile range (without air refueling) and carried 25,000 pounds of bombs, the weight equivalent of four Mark 15 megaton bombs.

10. Fusing was one of the most daunting of the technical challenges in the development of nuclear weaponry (after, of course, the production of the fissile material itself). That the Soviets could drop bombs "[fused] for air or surface burst or for delayed action" reveals a range of design capabilities far beyond the mere meaning of these words. To inflict widespread physical damage, a nuclear bomb would be fused for an airburst at between 800 to 1,600 feet above ground. The bombs dropped on Hiroshima and Nagasaki were airburst bombs. If contamination is the objective, or if the objective is to destroy an underground bunker, surface fusing is best. Surface detonations lift up the most radioactive material (which then contaminate the area) and craters deepest into the ground. (The Sedan crater at the Nevada Test Site is 320 feet deep.) Delayed fusing is another choice. Delayed fusing is a laydown bomb. It hits the ground, and waits. One reason for a laydown bomb is to delay the explosion (or explosions) long enough for the bombers to escape the target area.

2. Warning Capabilities:

a. Weapons launched from submarines may arrive without warning. Likewise, weapons emplaced by clandestine means may be detonated without warning.

b. An air defense warning of an initial mass attack by manned aircraft can be received on the Canadian border and the Atlantic, Pacific and Gulf coasts from a few minutes to three hours before the aircraft reach those boundaries. Intelligence as to the probable time attacking aircraft will take to reach specific areas can be available to civil defense through the Attack Warning System.

c. Interior areas can have one to three hours additional warning between the time an air defense warning is received and the time when they are under attack from manned aircraft.

d. Strategic warning cannot be assured.

See note #11, #12, #13 and #14

11. Surprise is the key word here. In a press conference, Dwight D. Eisenhower, then supreme commander of North Atlantic Treaty Organization (NATO) forces in Europe summed up what was a nationwide fear: "No man can know for sure at what hour, if ever, our defensive organization may be put to the ultimate test. Because our purpose is entirely defensive, we must be ready at the earliest possible moment. Only an aggressor could name the day and hour of attack."

America has relied on several warning systems, none of which were built at the time of this document. These were (and are) the Ballistic Missile Early Warning System (BMEWS) stations in Thule (Greenland), Alaska, and England; the Distant Early Warning (DEW) line; the Canadian Pinetree early warning radars; and the Navy's Ocean Picket line of ships. Today, of course, satellites would provide warning.

12. In 1958 little could forewarn when the *first* nuclear weapons that would hit America—these would be missiles launched from Soviet submarines or bombs hidden inside America. But what warning might have been possible? Historians have calculated some numbers. The warning one might expect before a submarine-launched ballistic missile impacted was in the range of 13 minutes. An airborne attack might be preceded by 25 minutes' warning. There would be no warning for a weapon preplaced on American soil. As early as 1958, American intelligence agencies had reason to believe that it was possible to smuggle a nuclear weapon into the United States, place it in a desired location, and then control its firing. This is information that has never before been released to the public.

13. The Soviets are expected to use all three arrows in their nuclear quiver: bombers, missiles, and submarines. The Soviet battle doctrine at the time called for fully engaged, penetrating, all-out attack in the first wave of any strike.

14. In response to the prospect of a surprise attack, SAC trained its forces to get off the ground and into the air in just 15 minutes. As remarkable as that may seem (and despite the obvious risks; many "ground alert" bombers crashed during their hastened departures), SAC was already experimenting with air alert bombers—nuclear bombers flying nuclear bombs, 24 hours a day, 7 days a week. SAC argued that it would be impossible for the Soviets to launch a decapitating first strike if enough bombers were always in the air and thus ready to strike back. This retaliatory capability was the underpinning to MAD—Mutually Assured Destruction. Military planners expected to expend their primary stores of nuclear weapons in the first three days of nuclear hostilities.

The Mark 15 nuclear bomb. The estimated yield
was 1.4 megatons.

The moment of detonation. These soldiers are in trenches 3,500 yards from ground zero. The light is from the flash of an atomic bomb. Even thus sheltered, many felt the "blowtorch-like" heat of the thermal pulse as it passed over their trench. Others likened the shock wave to the intense jolt of an earthquake.

PART I. PLANNING INFORMATION

B. MILITARY EFFECTS [was not released]

C. SITUATION ASSUMPTIONS

SITUATION ASSUMPTIONS are statements describing a national condition and a condition of the international political and military environment, the existence of which would require immediate and forceful action by the U.S. Government. They are not forecasts of future events but describe for planning purposes a condition that could occur.

The situation described herein has resulted from the exercise of *some* of the capabilities of the USSR described in Section A, CAPABILTY ASSUMPTIONS, and the effects of atomic weapons described in Section B, WEAPONS EFFECTS.

See note #15, #16, #17 and #18

15. The author makes it clear that the Situation Assumptions have two important characteristics: First, if the situations occurred as described, each situation would require a response by the United States. But, second, it was not necessarily true that these situations would actually come about. However, because each of the situations describes a nuclear strike against the United States, the then operable "forceful action" would have been a massive nuclear retaliation.

16. Our own counterpart to this strategy would be the SIOP—the Single Integrated Operating Plan. SIOP was instituted in 1960. The SIOP described a coordinated attack that combined the nuclear forces of the Army, Navy, and the Air Force.

17. Hydrogen bombs were so unspeakably destructive that one need possess only a small number to make large parts of the world uninhabitable. In one of the most important speeches of his presidency, Eisenhower appeared before the General Assembly of the United Nations on December 8, 1953, to voice his concerns. This speech came to be known as his "atoms for peace" speech. These new thermonuclear weapons, Eisenhower said to a hushed audience, were so powerful that either side could inflict "hideous damage" on the other. "No expenditure can guarantee the absolute safety for the cities and citizens of any nation," he said. Moreover, with bombs as large as these, and with the defensive measures then in place, the surviving retaliatory force of the United States would be so powerful that "an aggressor's land would be laid to waste."

As this speech was the first public acknowledgement of thermonuclear weapons. The audience was utterly silent. The two superpowers, said Eisenhower, were now nations that could "eye each other indefinitely across a trembling world" with weapons that would "annihilate" mankind and condemn it "to begin all over again the age-old struggle upward from savagery toward decency, justice and right."

18. This is the first reference to the missing section, I-B, Weapons Effects. This section would likely be a description of the blast as well as the thermal and radiation effects of nuclear strikes against military, industrial, and civilian targets. It would certainly include both the size of weapons expected and the number delivered by the Soviets against each ground zero. New York, for instance, might suffer the blows of a dozen 20-megaton thermonuclear bombs, while Ft. Knox might receive just one Hiroshima-sized kiloton bomb.

1. THE ATTACK

1. The USSR has made attacks with large numbers of atomic weapons on the United States and on some of its territories, bases overseas, and its Allies. The domestic air defense warning yellow for the first attack was disseminated two hours before USSR aircraft appeared over U.S. frontiers. At the same time as the air defense warning yellow was announced, submarine-launched missiles arrived and weapons emplaced by clandestine means were detonated. However, the major weight of attack has been delivered by manned aircraft.

See note #19 and #20

"...our land and naval

forces are heavily engaged."

19. In 1944, physicist James Franck headed a special committee of the Manhattan Project to consider the social and political implications of the atomic bomb. Said the report: "In no other type of warfare does the advantage lie so heavily with the aggressor."

20. Two remarkable statements are contained in the assumptions about the attack. The first is that we will go to "air defense warning yellow," presumably a level of heightened alert similar to our DefCon status levels. This means that the planners assumed that the attack would be preceded by diplomatic saber rattling or the evidence of some physical preparations by the Soviets—the amassing of ground forces near the German borders, for instance. However, whatever warning we have will be of little use: bombs are expected to detonate even as the warning is disseminated. According to these assumptions, the first flashes of light will be the detonation of submarine-launched ballistic missiles. Whatever condition merits "air defense warning yellow," Soviet submarines have already positioned themselves, unobserved, for the first wave. The second statement is interesting because, even as early as 1958, 40 years before the first terrorist bombing of the World Trade Center in New York, intelligence experts anticipated the clandestine use of atomic weapons. The next flashes would come from weapons secreted into the United States and covertly placed in strategic locations.

2. Air Defense operations in North America and overseas have destroyed a substantial portion of the attacking aircraft but half of those destroyed had reached the bomb release lines and had released their weapons. U.S. and Allied military operations have resulted in casualties and damage to the enemy at least as great as those received. Notwithstanding severe losses of military and civilian personnel and materiel, air operations against the enemy are continuing and our land and naval forces are heavily engaged. Both sides are making use of atomic weapons for tactical air support and in the land battle.

See note #21 and #22

21. This paragraph describes a violent war. The Army, Navy, and Air Force are leveling firepower against the Soviets, the scale of which would be unprecedented. By the end of 1957, SAC had 40 air wings with 3,128 bombers and fighters—2,000 of which were capable of carrying nuclear bombs, 5,543 of which were in our stockpiles. One must presume that the entirety of this force is in the battle. SAC is sending bombers to Russia; air defense squadrons are dog-fighting. How, though, would the combat (not the attacks) begin? Our first line of defense would be our air intercept fighters. An example would be the 444th Fighter Intercept Squadron of the 35th Air Division based at North Charleston Air Force Base, South Carolina. In 1958, flying the new, radar-equipped F-86L jets, the 444th and other squadrons would scramble to their jets and attack the first inbound bombers. Unfortunately, half of the Soviet planes that they do shoot down have already dropped their bombs. Thus the advantage of surprise. The jets flown by the 444th (and others) were some of the first jets equipped with air-to-air radars. The radars were primitive affairs prone to software failures, and required pilots to place their faces against a hood and steer a blip on the screen toward their target.

The United States still maintains alert and strip alert fighters. When pilots are on strip alert, they literally sit in the cockpit of their jets waiting for the go order. During the strikes against the World Trade Center in 2001, alert fighters scrambled but failed to reach their targets. It is unclear if any fighters were on that day sitting strip alert.

22. As we counterstrike, we will use nuclear weapons, some of which will explode in our own air space. The Genie air-to-air nuclear missile would be the "tactical air support" weapon referred to in paragraph 2. Genie was built on the interesting—although potentially outmoded—assumption that the invading Soviet bombers would fly in the tightly packed formations used in World War II. Genie, carried aloft by our fighter planes, would fire off a wing and streak into the center of such a formation and, so the theory continued, blast a dozen bombers out of the sky in one shot with its enormous shock wave. The Army had atomic weapons, too, and they are engaged in the battle. The author probably refers to the 280-mm shells fired from a nuclear artillery piece once dubbed "Atomic Annie." Annie's warhead yielded 15 kilotons. Genie was tested as the John shot in 1957 at the Nevada Test Site. It was much smaller; its yield is believed to have been to be 1 kiloton.

A live nuclear rocket is carried aloft by a F-89 Scorpion. The nuclear rocket project began in early 1954 and was code-named "Genie" by the USAF Air Research and Development Command. The flash of the exploding nuclear warhead was seen in the sky at 7:30 AM, July 19, 1957. This signaled the first time in aviation history that a live nuclear weapon was fired by a fighter aircraft. This is but one example of the tactical nuclear weapons mentioned in the doomsday scenario.

The Baker shot of Operation Crossroads. This underwater detonation contaminated almost all of the test fleet of mothballed ships. Similar underwater detonations are predicted in the doomsday scenario.

3. **The USSR is expected to use its remaining capability to launch additional strategic air attacks and has considerable air power for tactical and air defense operations.** The USSR submarine fleet is active in both the Atlantic and Pacific and serious losses to U.S. and Allied-controlled ocean shipping are being incurred. Intensive propaganda is being directed against the U.S. and its Allies. Clandestine activities and sabotage are being conducted.

4. **Both on the North American continent and overseas, the major weight of the attacks appears to have been directed on U.S. and Allied military installations including atomic weapons delivery capabilities and facilities producing atomic weapons, coastal naval bases, concentrations of ground forces, and ports and airfields servicing international transportation.** In addition, the District of Columbia and many population and industrial centers have been attacked. Due to actions of Air Defense Forces and to aiming and other errors of the attacking forces, many weapons resulted in random surface bursts.

See note #23 and #24

23. Bombs are dropping everywhere. Mushrooms clouds are rising over our military bases, our industrial bases, our manufacturing towns, our airports, and many other locations. Some bombs are falling randomly. Washington, D.C., is heavily hit (as would be expected). Civilian populations, however, do not seem to be targeted. Why did the planners presume this? The use of weapons against civilian populations is a tactic designed to break an opponent's will to fight, but it has rarely worked. The terrorist attacks of September 11 unified America and resolved a national will to strike back. The strikes against London during World War II strengthened the resolve of the British. The atomic strikes against Hiroshima and Nagasaki were more of a factor, but that action came at the end of protracted battles. Nonetheless, the national will would not have been a factor in the early stages of this nuclear war. Nuclear war would be automatic. Our battle doctrine at the time was to respond with massive and instant retaliation. Thus, the Soviets are furiously trying to destroy our capacity to retaliate. They are wasting no bombs on terror strikes.

Sabotage, though, is very much a factor. It was well known then and is well known now that the spy agencies of the eastern bloc actively infiltrated our nation. One of the more unusual tactics was to send students to our universities who were in fact operatives. Others were more mundane—operatives taking jobs in America or Americans recruited to be double agents. These "sleepers" have been activated and are now destroying what they can through sabotage.

24. The majority of the nuclear bombs are set for airbursts, but the attacks on our ports likely involved nuclear depth charges, nuclear torpedoes, and free-fall bombs. Underwater detonations, as we learned during the Baker shot of Operation Crossroads (1946) are among the dirtiest types of nuclear explosions. They generate a massive plume of water followed by a cloud of radioactive mist. The shroud of "hot" mist that rolled over the ships following Baker, which was an underwater explosion of an atomic bomb, did what Able, the airburst that preceded it, could not. Able sunk or destroyed only a few ships; Baker "fatally" contaminated over 100. Despite weeks, if not months, of wash-downs and scrubbing, most could not be decontaminated. Out of frustration, and to get rid of them, many were simply sunk.

An underwater nuclear bomb explodes and more than 2 million tons of water are lifted into the air. At the base of the column, a wall of radioactive mist and water begins to overrun the test ships arrayed around ground zero. This base surge is one of the deadliest forms of radioactive fallout.

The military conducted numerous effects tests. Here solders from the 1952 Desert Rock exercises examine a mannequin blown down by the shockwave and scorched by the thermal pulse 1700 yards from ground zero.

5. The weapons employed range from a few kilotons TNT equivalent to several megatons. All of the weapons in the megaton range burst on the surface. The great majority of the weapons in the kiloton range were air bursts. Blast and thermal radiation damage extends from 5 miles to as much as 15 miles from ground zeros. Severe fire storms have occurred in heavily built-up cities and many rural fires were started involving growing crops and forests. The surface bursts have resulted in widespread radioactive fallout of such intensity that over substantial parts of the United States the taking of shelter for considerable periods of time is the only means of survival. Prior to assurance of safety anywhere on the surface, without shelter, radiological defense monitoring is essential.

6. The general level of casualties throughout the United States is extremely serious. In many localities it is catastrophic. The following is an estimate as of D-Plus-7 of casualties which have occurred or will occur as a result of the attacks:

(Millions)

	Killed and Injured, Fatally Injured	Recovery Possible	Total
Blast and Thermal	12.5	12.5	25
Nuclear Radiation	12.5	12.5	25
Totals	25.0	25.0	50

Without thorough radiological defense monitoring and the application of adequate protective measures many more radiation injuries will occur from the cumulative effects of exposure to residual radiation and the consumption of contaminated foodstuffs and water.

See note #25

25. The population of the United States in 1958 was 140,000,000. Almost one in five will die.

Mannequins were used as stand-ins for humans during the civilian blast-effects tests conducted in Nevada. Two miles from ground zero, standard building materials provided sufficient protection to survive the shock wave and the thermal pulse, although, as this picture above suggests, injuries would be severe.

Within a mile of ground zero, armored personnel carriers, tanks, and self-propelled artillery all met with the same fate. Most were destroyed or rendered inoperable. In some cases, the heat of the thermal pulse caused the metal on the turret to fuse with the body of the tank. Nevada Test Site.

> *"Days, weeks and months must elapse before great areas are safe for continued occupancy."*

PART I. PLANNING INFORMATION

C. SITUATION ASSUMPTIONS

2. POST-ATTACK ANALYSIS

1. GENERAL. With human casualties exceeding material losses, ultimate recuperative potential to meet the requirements of the surviving population is high, providing this population can be adequately motivated. In spite of the magnitude of the catastrophe that has struck the nation and the possibility of additional, but lighter attacks, more than 100 million people and tremendous material resources remain. Restoration of the economy and our society will be possible and necessary. The speed with which restoration is accomplished will depend on governmental leadership and direction, maintenance of the confidence, and initiative of the people and the wisdom of the organization for utilization of remaining resources.

2. The attack has caused an almost complete paralysis in the functioning of the economic system in all of its aspects. For many years the size and shape of the economy will reflect these effects. There is an immediate severe impact on organized governmental activities, a fragmentation of society into local groups, a deterioration of our social standards, a breakdown in our system of exchange, and complete disruption of normal production processes. The functioning of the post-attack economy may depend chiefly on the rapidity and efficiency with which local and regional action can be organized to carry out broad national policies disseminated as widely as possible before attack — and reiterated or expanded by any means immediately after attack. This would naturally include the maximum utilization of our remaining resources, among other things.

See note #26 and #27

26. The rebuilding of America will be from the ground up—local, regional, and national—but it will begin with leadership. This section warns that survivors may be so dispirited by the carnage around them that it may be difficult, if not impossible, to motivate them. This was not the case in New York. When the twin towers of the World Trade Center collapsed, Americans from all over the nation streamed into New York to help.

27. This paragraph is eerily prescient. Following the September 11 strikes, the economy of the United States was virtually shut down. The New York Stock Exchange, NASDAQ, and the American Stock Exchange closed and didn't reopen until the following Monday. When they did, share prices plummeted. The airlines, which were grounded for almost a week, were financially decimated. Tourist destinations went begging for business. Retails stores saw their traffic dwindle to a trickle.

The Marines conduct maneuvers beneath a now diffused nuclear mushroom cloud. Nevada Test Site.

Soldiers look at ground zero during military maneuvers at the Nevada Test Site. The dark haze is not unlike that which one might expect to see shrouding a city after a Soviet strike. Desert Rock was designed to prove that a nuclear battlefield was no different from any other battlefield, if proper precautions were taken.

3. Consideration of the post-attack situation must be directed to two separate and distinct phases, although at some point in time these overlap and tend to merge. The first period might be described as predominantly the survival period; the second is predominantly the reconstruction period.

4. During the survival period the economy is operating in a highly disorganized manner. The utilized labor force is engaged in large numbers in disposing of the dead, taking care of surviving injured, decontaminating and cleaning up bombed areas, returning public works and utilities to operation, and other activities related to the direct and immediate effects of the attacks. After taking account of the armed forces requirements, the emergency government workers, and essential services, there are few workers left to produce goods. During the first three to six months there will be more capacity for the production of goods than workers to operate the facilities. The production of goods of any kind will be either of an emergency nature—essential survival items—or of a haphazard nature in isolated, not directly affected areas.

5. Protection of the whole population from the physiological effects of radioactive fallout is the most significant aspect of this period. Days, weeks and months must elapse before great areas are safe for continued occupancy. Many areas are of such importance that decontamination measures must be taken without waiting for radioactive delay.

6. The care of the surviving injured presents a major problem, calling for the coordination of all resources which can be used in this field. The

See note #28

28. The poststrike outlook is not unlike that of any national catastrophe. The first priority is to recover and care for the casualties, the "rescue" phase of a disaster. The second priority is to recover the dead and begin reconstruction. But this is not just a disaster. This is a nuclear disaster. In addition to rebuilding, a large number of people will be decontaminating areas vital to the reconstruction of America. Decontamination means washing down buildings, city blocks, ships, and airplanes—anything that is undamaged and needed for the recovery. It is a lengthy, risky business and success is not guaranteed.

The author describes a nation divided into three functions. Those who are able will remain in the military and will continue the battles. Another large percentage of the population will be treating the wounded and burying the dead. Others will decontaminate and restore factories and begin to get the wheels of the economy rolling.

The shock wave from the nearby atomic bomb has blown a Navy blimp out of the sky. Men mill about at the crash site. *Nevada Test Site*

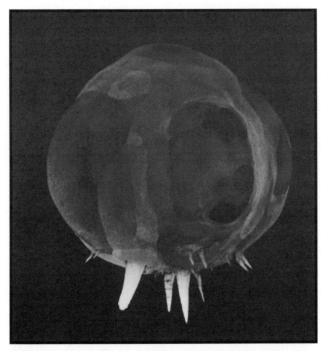

Filmed at 1/1,000,000 of a second, this is the initial pulse of an atomic explosion. The "fingers" protruding out of the fireball show how the blast traced down the guy wires of the tower in the instant before it vaporized the entire structure.

provision of the necessary food, clothing, and lodging also call for concentrated efforts on all governmental levels. The main problem with respect to food and clothing is one of distribution, arranging to get the available supplies to the areas of greatest needs. The main problem with respect to lodging is directing people to where lodging is available. Action during this survival period must be directed principally toward steps to ensure survival of the remaining population and support of necessary military operations.

7. After the more pressing of the survival needs of the damaged economy have been met, the reconstruction period will start. There will be an overlap here; the latter period will start before the former ends and it will be impossible to state precisely when one starts and the other stops. Basic actions necessary for re-establishment of the economy, particularly as to the undamaged parts, will have to be taken, announced, or stimulated at the earliest possible moment of the post-attack effort; although some longer-term actions in that connection may not become wholly relevant until the secondary stage.

8. The reconstruction phase calls for actions of a different type than those used in the survival phase. In the survival phase, the concern is for the immediate needs of the people; in the reconstruction phase, the emphasis is on programs for the future needs of the nation. In the light of the damage, the remaining resources, and the overall national demands, it must be decide[d] what programs must be started. During this period there will still be severe strains on

See note #29

29. The reconstruction phase will be hampered by the absence of infrastructure. Consider the economy today. Approximately 800,000 trucks will, on any one day, speed down our interstate highways at 70 miles per hour hauling goods from factory to distribution centers to warehouses to retail outlets. In the doomsday scenario, these roads and overpasses would be gone. Ground transportation will be hopelesly snarled. Manufacturing thus will be slowed too by the lingering contamination and an irregular and largely absent work force. Rail and air distribution, will be almost impossible (rail yards and airports would be targeted first). Moreover, the healthiest survivors may be hundreds of miles from where they're needed; yet even when they are found and recruited, they may be unwilling to leave their families and travel into the radiation zones.

Just as planners believed in the aftermath of the doomsday attack, stimulating the economy was exactly the blueprint for recovery in the aftermath of the September 11 attacks. President Bush, and a united Congress, quickly passed airline relief funding and pressed for legislation with other economic stimuli. The American people themselves came to the nation's aid. Over $1 billion in donations and countless liters of blood were received within 30 days of the tragedy.

resources, such as manpower, facilities, materials, and services. Programs for the maximum utilization of remaining resources must be devised.

9. GOVERNMENT. Governmental control is seriously jeopardized and central federal direction is virtually non-existent. Many of the highest government officials are casualties although the presidential office is functioning. Washington was so severely damaged that no operations there are possible. Token complements of personnel at the relocation centers for those governmental agencies that had them are inadequate to carry out essential functions. Some additional personnel who evacuated during the warning period or waited out the radiation hazard in adequate shelter will be available to augment the relocation complements where fallout conditions permit. Because of heavy fallout, none of the personnel at a few of the relocation sites survived. At several additional relocation sites almost all personnel are sick and many are dying. The same situation applies to the Regional Mobilization Committee headquarters. Communication and transportation between the relocation and regional centers are inadequate. In many areas, including several of the largest cities, where surviving injured outnumber the surviving uninjured active adults, the social fabric has ceased to exist in the pre-attack pattern. Confusion is widespread in these areas and customary control and direction are non-existent. These extreme conditions are most prevalent in the vicinity of the heavily damaged and contaminated areas.

See note #30, #31 and #32

76

30. From the IRS to the U.S. Post Office, virtually every federal agency had CoG plans; however, historians have roundly criticized them as being too far away to be reached in the event of a nuclear attack (most were 50 to 70 miles from Washington, D.C.), or too vulnerable to weapons effects. Here we see that even in 1958, the government actually agreed. Shelters would be inadequate. Many would be destroyed. Most were too far away to be useful; a large number for whom the shelters were intended would die before they reached them. Those who did get in would be so badly contaminated that they would soon succumb to radiation sickness and die.

Interestingly, the vulnerability of the relocation shelters was not lost on the Pentagon and alternate plans were already underway. Even as this document was being written, a fleet of 39 Airborne Command Post and two Navy ships were being commissioned as Emergency Command Posts. This is, however, the first written admission that "none of the personnel at a few of the relocation centers" survived.

31. The president survives. How that happens is unexplained; one is therefore tempted to write this off to hubris. Luck would be the most important factor. President Bush was in Florida when the terrorists struck on September 11. Passengers crashed the fourth plane before it hit its target. Was it aimed for the White House? As with any no-notice attack, those who live owe their lives as much to luck as planning.

32. Once again, the author refuses to gloss over the human price of this tragedy. In the cities, he notes, the surviving injured outnumber the surviving uninjured. Confusion reigns. Social order has ceased.

A sub-surface burst seen from about 12 miles away. This 1955 photo amply illustrates why a surface explosion is so deadly. The dust and sand are radioactive, and will cause widespread contamination to the local area. *Nevada Test Site*

Mannequins in the assembly area prior to Operation Doorstep.
As part of a series of civil defense tests, they were placed in
frame houses, autos, and shelters arrayed around ground zero.

10. HEALTH. Health resources, including physicians, nurses, and other manpower, hospitals and other medical care facilities, and health supplies and equipment, are in a critical state. This results both from the high concentration of these resources in the attacked areas, and from the unprecedented requirements for the surviving resources. Even with the most stringent selection of patients to be treated, rationing of supplies from the outset, and maximum support of industrial restoration, remaining supplies will be adequate only for minimal needs.

11. From a pre-attack total of 1.6 million hospital beds, approximately 100,000 are available for use at D-7. Where medical care is possible, most patients are being treated under improvised arrangements—on the ground, in tents, in any available buildings—utilizing civil defense emergency hospitals and other available hospitals and medical equipment.

12. The patient load requirements have essentially exhausted immediately available health and sanitation supplies in the affected areas. Much of the supplies remaining are either inaccessible or unusable because of radiological contamination or because of the disruption of transportation. The production potential for health supplies and equipment is almost completely inoperable for an extended period. Most of the plants which remain are seriously damaged or inactivated due to radioactive contamination and lack of skilled personnel.

See note #33 and #34

> *"Because of the heavy fallout, none of the peronnel at a few of the relocation sites survived."*

33. The author acknowledges that the surviving injured may not receive medical care even if they do reach a treatment facility. Ninety percent of the hospital beds in the nation are destroyed. Burn cases would be numerous, and also the hardest to treat. Burns are a specialty in medicine. Treatment in 1958 was in no way sophisticated. Burns infect easily. The pain is great. Burn centers are few. In recent years, a group called the Physicians for a Responsible World warned that a single nuclear bomb exploded in New York City would produce more burn patients than all the burn beds in the nation.

34. Antibiotics are running low; no new manufacturing is expected. "Even with the most stringent selection of patients to be treated," says the document, medical resources will be inadequate. Triage is an accepted practice in medical emergencies. Those too injured to save would be left to die. Those who are unable to be treated may not even have the small comfort of morphine or some other pain relief.

These Rad-Safe Technician Monitors wash down after examining ground zero. *Nevada Test Site.*

T-33 jet aircraft were among the types of jets used to collect samples of the radioactive residues inside a nuclear mushroom cloud. Here, men remove the samples from the aircraft and package them for shipment to an Atomic Energy Commission laboratory for radiochemical analysis. These men were part of the unique Filter Recovery Unit of the Air Force. The wingtip pod in the background carries the special filters aloft.

13. The medical care requirements are overwhelming. In addition to 25,000,000 dead or dying, there are 25,000,000 surviving casualties who require emergency medical care. Of this number, one-half (12,500,000) are suffering from blast and thermal injuries and have an immediate and evident need for treatment. Of the 25,000,000 radiation casualties, 12,500,000 have received lethal dosages and have died or will die regardless of treatment. Of the 12,500,000 remaining one-half will require hospitalization at some time during the period from D-2 weeks to D-12 weeks, with the peak, 5,000,000 being reached between D-5 weeks and D-7 weeks. Some of this requirement for hospitalization can be met by facilities becoming available which were earlier unusable due to contamination and shortages of transportation and other services.

14. Inadequate provision for laboratory diagnostic aids has hampered the more accurate determination of degrees of radiation injury. Unless such determinations are made, many lives may be lost because treatment is being given to hopeless cases.

15. Besides the casualties resulting from the effects of attack—blast, thermal, and nuclear radiation—there are 120 million surviving of which there is a daily census of 9 million (on the basis of a threefold increase over normal peacetime experience) requiring some type of medical care

See footnote #35 and #36

35. Sadly, radiation sickness is one of the most painful ways to die, yet the doomsday scenario says that more than 12 million Americans have received lethal doses. There is no known cure, no way to reverse its course, and precious little human data. What is known is not good. Twice men were exposed to lethal does of radiation, both in the mid-1940s. Both occurred at in the nuclear labs at Los Alamos, New Mexico. One of these men, Louis Slotin, died within nine days of his exposure. The other, Harry Daghlian, died within 25 days. Daghlian understood the medical significance of his exposure and allowed photographers to chronicle his deterioration. His hand was photographed. It was seared and the flesh was burnt away, the tissue swollen to the bursting point. The rest of the photographs have not been released.

36. Many radiation victims die of gastrointestinal damage. Gamma rays work best on soft tissue, the type of tissue in the intestine. Gastrointestinal Syndrome (GIS) is a painful condition seen in only in a few heavily irradiated laboratory animals, and the survivors of Hiroshima and Nagasaki.Radiation victims experience extreme gastrointestinal pain and are likely to slough their gut.

The military tested a wide variety of shelters for soldiers on the nuclear battlefield. These simple lean-tos, trees, and even fog was effective if one was far enough away from ground zero. Tests such as these helped dispel the myth that nuclear weapons were omnipotent.

The survivability of food in the event of nuclear war was a concern to civilian planners in the 1950s. This larder, kept in one of the test houses, was nicknamed "Grandma's Pantry." After the bomb blasts penetrated the test houses, scientists would examine these pantries to determine the durability of food packaging and the degree of radioactivity present in the foods. Operation Doorstep, Annie shot, Nevada Test Site.

because of displacement of people, disruption of normal medical and sanitation services, pollution of food and water supplies, environmental exposure, physical and emotional stress, malnutrition and overcrowding. Included in the 9 million above, the numbers afflicted with communicable diseases are considered to be increasing rapidly among both the adult and the pre-adult populations. These diseases include typhoid fever, influenza, smallpox, diphtheria, tetanus, and diarrheal and streptococcal diseases. There are some reports of outbreaks of yellow fever and other tropical diseases in the South and of plague, cholera, and typhus in coastal cities. Reserve stocks of vaccines are being rapidly depleted or are inaccessible due to fallout, blast damage, or other reasons. Epidemics of certain of these and of other communicable diseases are anticipated.

16. FOOD. Many survivors will need to remain under cover and acute shortages will develop except in the available shelters that have been equipped by individuals or groups with adequate food and supplies. When decay of radioactivity permits movement of people out of shelters in the contaminated areas, it is important that food supplies be available without delay. Salvable food stocks in the contaminated areas will particularly meet immediate needs since requirements have been reduced by heavy loss of life. To make up local deficiencies, additional food must be shipped into some areas. Ability to do this depends on adequacy of transportation and communication since food supplies in the nation as a whole are expected to be adequate for all essential civilian and military needs in this immediate post-attack period. Day

See note #37

"Many of the highest government officials

are casualties."

37. Following the medical crisis will be a food crisis. Even a well-stocked fallout shelter (and many public and private shelters were) will run dry of foodstuffs. At that point, the problem is contamination and distribution. Foods fit for human consumption will not necessarily be located in or near the ground zeros, yet transportation to and from the war zones will be spotty. Furthermore, those unable to test foodstuffs risk the potentially lethal consequences of ingesting radioactive meats, poultry, grains, or fluids. Washing contaminated food can help, and so it is likely that the government would be actively broadcasting information about how to "clean" food. It is also likely that the military would soon be airlifting supplies and parachuting them into population clusters.

to day production of essential food commodities must be maintained and, where necessary, restored, since existing food stocks cannot for long make up for loss of current production.

17. HOUSING AND COMMUNITY FACITITIES. The housing situation is critical. Fire and blast have either completely destroyed or rendered unrepairable significant portions of the housing supply. The situation is further complicated by fallout which has made much of the remaining housing unusable for varying lengths of time. In only very isolated situations is the housing inventory adequate to rehouse survivors from attacked areas. Extensive repair and restoration work on the remaining standing stock and emergency shelters are desperately needed. Voluntary and enforced billeting measures and utilization of non-residential structures are being effected.

18. Community facilities have been extremely hard hit. Blast damage has not only completely eliminated major water and sewer networks, but has at the same time dangerously impaired the function of water and sewer facilities in peripheral areas otherwise unaffected by blast and fire damage. Stopgap arrangements for providing potable water from local sources are in effect, but waste disposal is a serious health menace.

See note #38 and #39

> *"Bartering, unorganized confiscation and looting are in evidence and threaten further the restoration of any orderly degree of economic activity."*

38. The thermal pulse will vaporize or burn everything within a mile of ground zero. Here are some data. A 10-megaton nuclear bomb will produce second-degree burns (blisters) on exposed flesh 20 miles from ground zero. In these paragraphs we read that the housing situation is critical. Does the author contradict an earlier assumption and now say that civilian populations were targeted? Probably not. But collateral damage in nuclear war would be unavoidable and extensive.

39. This section is overly dramatic. Nuclear bombs, while potent, are not, in small numbers, capable of large-scale geographic destruction. This was proved at the test sites. The effects of atomic and nuclear bombs were tested on homes, mock factories, fuel storage facilities, fallout shelters, radio towers, and more. Even rows of different types of fabrics were arrayed around ground zero, as well as mannequins held upright by poles. Trains were placed around ground zero, as were cars, airplanes, bombers, artillery pieces, and even mock-soldiers lying on the ground. At least two films were released to the public by the Department of Energy and the Department of Defense (many more were made but were classified and shown only to those with security clearances). These films, called *Let's Face It* and *Operation Doorstep*, show the effects, bad and good. Distance remains the criti-

(continued on page 93)

"Fire and blast have either completely destroyed or rendered unrepairable significant portions of the Housing supply."

Frame houses were exposed to the blast and heat from an atomic bomb on March 17, 1953 at the Nevada Test Site. These houses were part of a Federal Civil Defense Administration safety program. This is a photo of house #1 located 3,500 feet from ground zero. The house was destroyed 2-1/3 seconds after the atomic blast. The camera was enclosed in a 2-inch lead sheath as a protection against radiation. The only source of light was that from the bomb. Many of the photographs from ground zero were made by Edgerton, Germehausen and Grier, Inc. (EG&G) for the AEC.

(continued from page 91)

cal factor in atomic war. Trees alone provide shelter enough to survive—if you're far enough away. Soldiers huddled in trenches just 2,500 yards from ground zero survived and even mounted a mock "attack" on ground zero. As few as a thousand yards often spelled the difference between a car that flipped and rolled over, and one that was largely unaffected. One could be 3 miles from a kiloton bomb and, if sheltered by a hill, have no ill effects. Remaining 8 miles away from an even larger bomb was so useless as a military indoctrination experience during the Operation Desert Rock exercises, that generals recommended moving the soldiers forward.

This section makes survival seem unlikely and yet the data from the test site says otherwise. Hills, dales, valleys, and even the simple distance of a Nebraska plain would shelter a home and its occupants.

The point is, nuclear weapons are like all weapons—they had finite kill radiuses, finite destruction rings, and finite uses in war scenarios. The real worry is radiation. Radiation continues the killing long after the military objective has been achieved. But even radiation is finite. The two largest thermonuclear bombs America exploded—Mike and Bravo— were both 10 megatons or larger. The fallout cloud from Mike was never found. Bravo, which contaminated the islands of Rongelab and Rongerik, spread over a 5,000-mile area but the contamination was in most cases less than a few rads.

19. MONETARY AND CREDIT SYSTEMS. The monetary and credit systems have collapsed in damaged areas and are under severe pressure in those areas overrun with refugees and in the areas where evacuees are concentrated. In transactions occurring in these areas the price structure is rising sharply as to some essentials while collapsing as to other goods and services. Bartering, unorganized confiscation, and looting are in evidence and threaten further the restoration of any orderly degree of economic activity. Because of the interrelationship of the monetary and banking systems, personal and business financial transactions in undamaged areas threaten to reach a standstill.

20. DOMESTIC COMMERCIAL COMMUNICATIONS. Minimum nationwide telephone and telegraph facilities remain available to provide for the exchange of urgent communications except with those areas actually bombed and destroyed, and with those areas in which communications facilities have been sabotaged. The loss of commercial power sources together with a serious personnel problem created by loss of specialized manpower through casualties, sickness and confusion, the fear of fallout, and lack of food and water, seriously limits employing the remaining communication facilities to their full capacity. Consequently, there are long delays in placing all but the most urgent telephone calls as well as in the delivery of telegraph messages.

See note #40 and #41

40. Refugees are a well-known by-product of war. Again, it is likely that a considerable effort will be made by the military to provide distribution (either through air drops or ground transportation) of currency and supplies. That said, this section assumes social disorder, a popular theme in doomsday books and end-of-the-world science fiction movies. Would that happen today? Perhaps, but little looting was in evidence on September 11.

41. Our nation's communication infrastructure has improved dramatically since this scenario was written, but it still has significant weaknesses. Consider the aftermath of September 11. As word of the disaster spread, phone circuits bogged down and telephone calls were either delayed or impossible to make. Cell tower capacity was maxed out. Even Internet traffic at news sites slowed to a crawl. Despite all the fiber in the ground, and all of the advances in telecommunications, the nation's communication infrastructure is still vulnerable, not just to bombs but to the loads placed on them by users.

Mannequins mounted against poles were exposed to the thermal effects of a bomb. A 10-kiloton bomb could produce flash burns 1.5 miles from ground zero. A 10-megaton bomb would have the same effect on skin 20 miles away. Data on the resistance of different fabrics to heat was studied in the aftermath. *Nevada Test Site*

A mannequin leans away from ground zero but is otherwise relatively intact. This mannequin was mummy-wrapped to minimize exposed skin. Flash burns, which are classified as second-degree burns, occur on exposed skin but are generally prevented by clothing.

21. INTERNATIONAL COMMERCIAL COM-
MUNICATION. International radiotelegraph,
radiotelephone, and cable control terminals located in gateway cities on the East and West
coasts have been destroyed. Damage from sabotage has occurred at cable landing locations
on both the East and West coasts and the cut-
ting of the ocean telephone cable has severely
reduced the submarine cable capacity for handling telegraph and telephone traffic to Atlantic, Hawaiian, and Alaskan points. Limited
radiotelegraph and radiotelephone capacity remains, however, but is unreliable due to electronic jamming, damage to facilities at overseas
locations, sabotage efforts, and radiological
contamination effects upon surviving technical
and operating personnel. Air mail is being employed where available and practicable to supplement the reduced capabilities of the overseas
communications network.

22. TRANSPORTATION. Severe disruption to
transportation service exists in all attacked and
contaminated areas. Within these areas there
has been heavy damage to terminal, warehousing,
servicing, and related facilities. Motor vehicles
in non-attacked areas free of contamination, including those not previously engaged in common carrier service, are being mustered for use
in support of disaster areas. Rail transportation
is affected more seriously by disruption of lines
and yards in attacked areas than by loss of
rolling stock. Large quantities of rail and highway motive power and equipment were not

See note #42 and #43

> *"The surface bursts have resulted in*
> *widespread radioactive fallout of such*
> *intensity that over substantial parts of the U.S.*
> *the taking of shelter for considerable periods*
> *of time is the only means of survival."*

42. Transportation is the backbone of commerce, and speed is the backbone of transportation. One need only suffer the long delays of a lane closure on the interstate highway system to picture what chaos would ensue when overpasses and bridges collapse. The military's resources would be essential to the reconstruction. True then. True now.

43. The U.S. Postal Service had rather formidable postnuclear attack responsibilities. One of them was to identify survivors and process change-of-address forms. In the war zones, few streets would survive as previously identified. Hundreds of thousands of Americans would be dislocated and would become refugees. The U.S. Post Office is expected to monitor the constant movement of survivors, create new addresses for them, and get the mail through.

damaged, making it possible to continue minimum essential traffic within those areas not duly affected by contamination and to restore principal lines to service as rapidly as radioactive decay or decontamination measures permit opening uncontaminated lines which bypass the physically damaged areas. However, reserve stocks of operating supplies and fuel for all forms of domestic transportation are being depleted at a faster rate than they are being replenished.

23. In major port areas there has been heavy damage to piers, warehousing, shipbuilding and repair yards, and related facilities. Damage to shoreside cargo handling facilities has necessitated the use of alternate outloading ports and sites along the coasts and the limitation of shipments to the current capacity of those locations. Damage to reserve fleets has been minor, but reactivation is impeded by losses of repair yards, tugs, and manpower. The worldwide distribution of merchant shipping at sea and in foreign ports has left the major part of the active fleet intact, but ship losses are nevertheless serious in light of immediate and heavy requirements for shipping to support and reinforce overseas military operations. Neither ships nor convoy protection in the vulnerable coastwise sea-lanes can be provided for other than direct military support, except in cases of extreme necessity in priority higher than that of the military. Merchant shipping, therefore, cannot be counted on to supplement or replace inland domestic surface transportation to any substantial extent.

The USS *Saratoga* slips beneath the waters inside Bikini lagoon seven hours after the underwater explosion of an atomic bomb. The rest of the fleet was extensively contaminated.

Ships arranged closest to ground zero suffered near-total topside damage. If not sunk outright, the ships were nearly molten from bow to stern. Able shot, Operation Crossroads, 1946.

A ten megaton bomb has the destructive force of 22 billion pounds of TNT. With megaton weapons, observers were often kept more than 100 miles from ground zero for safety.

24. Domestic airlift capacity has been decreased substantially due to damage and destruction of airfields, airstrips and aircraft, lack of communications, manpower, repair parts, fuel, and maintenance facilities. The remaining aircraft are largely devoted to high-priority routes and highest-priority traffic under the air priority system and other controls. Trans-ocean airlift capacity is decreased substantially due to destruction of aircraft, damage to bases, circuitous reroutings and inadequate ground facility capability.

25. ELECTRIC POWER. Due, for the most part, to heavy damage to distribution lines and substations in bombed cities, sufficient electric power is not immediately available in the majority of the fringe areas and reception centers for evacuees. Most acute need for power in such areas is for refrigeration, hospital operation, community water systems, heating, and mass feeding. Small portable generators can meet only a fraction of these needs. Aggregate generating capacity of electric utilities operable following the attack is sufficient for minimal national needs; therefore, the power shortage will be alleviated in most areas as soon as transmission and distribution lines can be repaired, new lines strung, interconnections effected and communications restored. Restoration of electric service will be slower than in cases of natural disaster. Anticipated delays are

See note #44 and #45

"The utilized labor force is engaged in large numbers in disposing of the dead...."

44. Contamination and risky sea-lanes lie at the core of transportation problems. Many ships will survive the strikes, but Soviet forces will remain on the attack. As attractive as it appears to be, it would not be possible to shift goods from trucks to the ocean until an armistice is signed.

45. The airlines were the first to be affected after the September 11 attacks. The next was consumer confidence and/or interest in traveling. Airlift capacity may be diminished, as the author states in 1958, but the need for airlift, especially transpacific or transatlantic, is questionable. Who would want to travel after the war?

due to several factors, including difficulty in transporting utility repair crews and material from undamaged areas to augment those in areas of need and denial of immediate access into fall-out areas to make repairs and to obtain stocks of materials and equipment, new or salvable. Where primary sources of steam-generated electric power have been destroyed, the power-consuming facilities (industrial plants, stores, homes, etc.) have, in large measure, likewise been destroyed. In most cases, where hydroelectric-generating facilities have been damaged, there is enough generating capacity intact in the system and through interconnections with other systems, to meet essential needs of the areas served. In those areas, however, sharp curtailment of supply to undamaged industrial plants will be necessary for an extended period. Enough skilled manpower has survived to operate generating plants. Fuel stocks at thermal generating plants using coal, are adequate to keep plants operating for a minimum of 30 to 60 days even after allowance for possible use of a part of their stockpiles for other emergency purposes. Generating plants dependent solely on oil as a fuel can continue operating for a shorter period from stocks on hand, the time varying with the stock position of individual plants.

This B-17 bomber was snapped in two, three miles from ground zero. Note the portions of its skin that were vaporized by the heat.

26. FUELS. Of all the fuels (including petroleum products, gas, and solid fuels), motor fuels including aviation are the most universally used throughout the nation, regardless of season. Therefore, even though movement of the mass of civilian passenger automobiles is strictly limited, the availability of motor fuels for uses essential to human survival and military operations is of widespread and urgent concern. Among such uses are the operations of trucks, diesel locomotives, water transport, aircraft, tractors and other farm equipment needed for food production, and a host of engines required for water supply, sanitary disposal systems, and hospitals.

27. Initial military operations are being fueled almost entirely from stocks in military storage. Stocks in motor fuels in undamaged areas to and through which evacuees moved are nearly exhausted, despite rationing efforts by some local authorities. In many of these areas and in contiguous support areas, radioactive fallout temporarily immobilizes all transport and farming operations, thus halting consumption in wheeled equipment and simultaneously preventing replenishment of stocks. When decay of fallout permits resumption of human activity, some consumers such as railroads, airlines, and to a lesser extent, certain farmers, can operate for a brief period using stocks on hand. Generally, however, there will be an immediate, heavy drain on bulk plant stocks of motor fuels including aviation. The rate at which such stocks can in turn be replenished will vary by areas, depending upon availability of surface transportation, the extent to which they are normally served by pipelines, and proximity to surviving, operable petroleum refineries.

See note #46 and #47

"Fire and blast have either completely destroyed or rendered unrepairable significant portions of the Housing supply."

46. In an otherwise dismal poststrike world, fuels would be available, albeit on a limited basis and often in hard-to-reach places. Power plants, motorized vehicles, even airplanes will resume limited, emergency operations from available stocks. The long-term prognosis, however, is not addressed. Presumably, enough oil could be imported after the war or the domestic oil fields could be reinvigorated within a reasonable amount of time.

47. The author points to the drop in demand for fuels resulting from the destruction of military equipment, and homes and buildings. Not factored in is the absence of any real desire to travel. Fuel prices plummeted in the aftermath of September 11 as more people stayed close to home.

28. In cold areas to and through which evacuees have moved, the situation with respect to cooking and heating fuels (kerosene, fuel oil, liquefied petroleum gas, coal, and gas) is somewhat similar to that of motor fuels. Sheltering and feeding of swollen populations in such areas are rapidly depleting cooking and heating fuels in homes and other buildings and, in communities served by natural gas, lowering pressure in distribution lines. Fallout prevents immediate replenishment of home stocks. When deliveries can be resumed, local distributors' stocks of fuel oil, "bottled" gas, and coal will soon be gone. Local industrial and some utility stockpiles of coal can be tapped if needed for heating of hospitals, homes, and shelters. Shifts from less available to more available fuels will be necessary. At the outset, wood where available is providing essential warmth, but this cannot long meet needs of masses of people. Again, provision of minimum essential supplies of cooking and heating fuels will depend largely upon restoration of transportation and communication.

Soldiers gather in trenches prior to a nuclear test at the Nevada Test Site. One could survive multikiloton explosions as close as 2,500 yards from ground zero, if dug deep enough into the ground.

29. The physical productive capacity of oil and gas wells and coal mines has been little affected by the attack, but their operation in some areas is precluded temporarily by radioactive fallout making surface work hazardous to human survival. Even after decay of fallout permits men to work at these facilities, breaks in power service will temporarily prevent operation of certain of them as well as some pipeline pumping stations. A substantial percentage of aboveground fuel facilities in bombed areas—including petroleum refineries, pipeline terminals, tank farms for storage of crude oil and products, gas compressor stations, and coal-handling equipment at rail and port terminals—have been destroyed or extensively damaged. Destruction of docks, tanks, and refineries in coastal areas has drastically curtailed inter-coastal movement and importation of petroleum and petroleum products by tankers. Inland, the disruption of and damage to railroad, waterway, and highway transport at or near urban centers will continue to hamper distribution of both coal and petroleum products.

30. The non-military requirements for fuel in the post-attack period will be much smaller than pre-attack requirements, since millions of fuel-consuming units—particularly residences, commercial buildings, electric power and generating plants, and factories—have disappeared in the bombing. With strict rationing of petroleum products and allocation of coal, the surviving fuel production capacity, including petroleum refinery capacity, is sufficient to meet properly

Decontaminating the engine on a B-50 bomber following aerial cloud sampling. Nevada Test Site.

time-phased military requirements and minimum essential civilian needs for both motor fuel and heating fuel and, also, progressively to supply reviving industries. Priority will be given to the supplying of fuel for human survival and military operations, including communications, transportation, electric power, and food production essential to both. Refinery yields will be adjusted to fit the pattern of needs for particular petroleum products depending on the season of the attack and military requirements. Nevertheless, due mainly to transportation difficulties, severe, localized shortages of one fuel or another from time to time during the next several months should be anticipated. This will call for endurance by affected communities, maximum conservation of motor fuels, perhaps a return to relatively primitive methods of cooking and heating, and ingenuity on the part of the fuel industries and government to alleviate shortages.

31. MANPOWER. In assessing the survival and emergency work to be done, total manpower requirements for civil defense purposes substantially exceed the available supply. Although manpower priorities have been established in individual local areas, the difficulties of communicating with higher levels of government have resulted in conflicting demands on certain support areas. Some civil defense services are experiencing support surpluses while others cannot function because needed support is lacking.

Wind has already sheared the steam of this mushroom cloud as it rises from the Nevada desert. Surface bursts intensify the local contamination whereas airbursts tend to suck up material from the ground and transport the ensuing fallout downwind.

32. The provision of effective manpower support is jeopardized by the dislocation and disorganization of the general population. In many communities evacuation took place in anticipation of initial and follow-up attack. They are now attempting to return to their homes but the process is slow, and previously identified skills cannot be located until the evacuated population is reestablished in the home community. It will be some time before manpower in such areas can be organized to provide needed support to devastated areas and to restore essential services and production.

33. In many localities radioactive fallout, the imminence of fallout, and particularly the fear of this unseen hazard has temporarily immobilized a tremendous proportion of the manpower which would otherwise be immediately available. Denial of access to large areas because of the fallout hazard has compounded the already major problems in transportation of labor to the point of need.

34. In many localities there is a surplus of manpower in certain skilled occupations which could be used if necessary equipment and supplies were available. In other localities, the best use of manpower resources requires the temporary separation of workers from their families until housing, transportation, feeding, and other conditions permit reuniting family groups wherever the workers are most needed. Difficulty has been encountered in trying to contain

The heat pulse from an atomic bomb has ignited the tires of this test automobile placed near ground zero. Nevada Test Site.

evacuated populations in relocation centers around cities which have been attacked so that they do not further endanger their lives by moving into fallout areas. Many thousands of people are trying to reach the homes of friends and relatives. As a consequence, the size of the labor force and the skill distribution within the relocated area changes continuously. The instability of this situation adversely affects the recruitment of specific skills within the area, and throws askew the labor assessments necessary to balance manpower demand with available supply with a minimum of population shift.

35. In relocation areas, utilization of available unskilled manpower for necessary emergency work is most inefficient for lack of enough trained civil defense technicians and of leaders and sub-leaders previously trained and organized.

36. Training programs offer little solution except for very short-term skill development.

37. PRODUCTION. As in all other areas of economic activity the effect of the attack on levels of production can best be described in time phases. There is an immediate and virtually complete paralysis of the production effort, even in non-damaged and slightly damaged areas. Following this "shock" phase, the gradual return of workers to their places of employment sets in motion a slow recovery cycle, manifesting itself first in scattered, undamaged, non-fallout areas. As the fallout decays and decontamination is started the areas of recovery expand, limited primarily by manpower shortages.

See note #48 and #49

48. Manpower is addressed on several occasions. Skilled laborers are not necessarily where they are needed. This was observed in New York City.The reallocation of workers was smoother and faster in 2001 than than it would have been in 1958.

49. The key word here is the "shock" phase. Yes, production will be curtailed or blocked due to damage, manpower losses, and radiation. But the "X" factor is the will of America to get back on its feet. Again, our experiences with the September 11 attacks are useful. There was a shock phase. It took time to get Americans back to work. It took encouragement. Government officials urged Americans to resume their normal lives. Comedians were urged to return to their TV shows. However awkward it was during those first few days, America did it. Within a month, there was some semblance of normalcy. Therein lies the great strength of America: the refusal to backslide into the abyss.

America's cultural heritage, although not specifically addressed in the *Emergency Plans Book*, was at considerable risk, too. The National Park Service formulated a plan to snatch and hold safe the Liberty Bell. The National Archives had special vaults to enclose the Declaration of Independence and the Bill of Rights. Both the National Gallery of Art and the General Services Administration developed an evacuation plan. Priceless paintings would be hurried out of Washington, D.C., and sheltered in a facility on the campus of Randolph-Macon College in Lynchburg, Tennessee.

The point is, America will rebuild—even after the doomsday attack. It is our nature.

38. During the early post-attack period primary emphasis must be placed on the production of essential civilian goods and services and on military items urgently needed for combat and support. Two major factors determine achievable levels of production.

39. First, a major limitation on post-attack production will arise from the damage to the chain of production. The pre-attack production levels achieved in this country resulted from the functioning of a highly complex operation, in which many thousands of contributors to overall production were bound together through the interrelationships of production processes. Suppliers of raw materials, fabricators of metal shapes and forms, manufacturers of components and subassemblies, and final product producers, all contributed to the flow of production in such a manner that, by and large, items necessary for successive steps in the productive process were available when and where needed. It is impossible to measure the damage to this chain of

Army soldiers defend positions near ground zero during exercises with a live atomic bomb. Nevada Test Site.

production in all of its ramifications. It seems reasonable to assume, however, that the process has suffered severe damage, not immediately reparable. It will take months to determine the bottlenecks and dislocations, and many more months to overcome shortages and imbalances. The resumption of any sizeable production effort will, of course, be dependent on the extent to which necessary services—power, transportation, communications, etc.—can be provided.

40. A second major limitation is the number and types of workers available for production purposes, particularly in the first six months. As the need for workers for emergency civil defense efforts lessens, more persons will become available for the production of goods and services. However, even after the first six months, manpower will still impose a restriction on the size of the production program, because of manpower losses and also because of the lowered efficiency of the available utilized labor force.

Soldiers board trucks after conducting exercises at the base of a nuclear explosion.

REFERENCES

General Accounting Office, *Continuity of Government in a Critical National Emergency*, Office of the Assistant to the President for Communications, Jimmy Carter Library.

National Security Memorandum No. 127, *Emergency Planning for Continuity of Government*, 1962, Special Assistant to the President for National Security Affairs, John Fitzgerald Kennedy Library.

National Security Memorandum No. 200, *Acceleration of Civil Defense Activities*, 1962, Special Assistant to the President for National Security Affairs, John Fitzgerald Kennedy Library.

U.S. Civil Defense Policy, 1984, National Security Council, Ronald Reagan Library.

The National Archives, RG 340, *Records of the Office of the Secretary of the Air Force, Secretary of the Air Force's security-classified general correspondence* (decimal), 1947–1954 (693 feet, *and top-secret general correspondence* (numerical), 1956–1964 (7 feet).

Executive Order 12148, *Federal Emergency Management Agency*, President Jimmy Carter, July 20, 1979.

Presidential Decision Directive, NSC-67, *Enduring Constitutional Government and Continuity of Government Operations*, 1998, President William Jefferson Clinton.

United Press International, *Hanssen Accused of Compromising Presidential Survival Plans*, New York, 2001, via Newsmax.com Wires.

Strategic Air Command, *The SAC Alert Program*, 1960, Headquarters, Strategic Air Command, Offutt, Nebraska.

Ben Rich and Leo Janis, *Skunk Works*, 1994, Little Brown, New York.

James N. Gibson, *Nuclear Weapons of the United States*, 1996, Schiffler Publishing, Ltd., Atglen, Pennsylvania.

Stephen I. Schwartz, *Atomic Audit*, 1998, The Brookings Institution, Washington, D.C.

David Donald and Jon Lake, editors, *The Encyclopedia of World Military Aircraft*, 1994, Aerospace Publishing, Ltd., London, England.

Rachel Fermi and Esther Samra, *Picturing the Bomb*, 1995, Harry N. Abrams, Inc., New York.

Mike Hill, John M. Campbell, and Donna Campbell, *Peace Was Their Profession. SAC: A Tribute*, 1995, Schiffler Publishing, Ltd., Atglen, Pennsylvania.

The Society of the Strategic Air Command, Strategic Air Command, not dated, Turner Publishing Company, Paducah, Kentucky.

Atoms For Peace, address by President Eisenhower before the United Nations.

A lean-to fallout shelter is tested during the Annie shot at the Nevada Test Site.

INDEX